June 10th Purchased at Bob's ECRTA Program "1993"

COUNTY ROAD
13

*Best Wishes &
John DeWees!
fellow teacher
Bob Baker*

Amm

COUNTY ROAD
13

Robert J. Baker

Foreword by J. Lorne Peachey

HERALD PRESS
Scottdale, Pennsylvania
Waterloo, Ontario

Library of Congress Cataloging-in-Publication Data
Baker, Robert J., 1920-
    Count road 13 / Robert J. Baker ; foreword by J. Lorne
Peachey.
        p.   cm.
    ISBN 0-8361-3540-7
    1. Christian life—Mennonite authors.   2. Conduct of life.
3. Baker, Robert J., 1920-   I. Title: County road 13.
BV4501.2.B38155   1990
248.8'5—dc20   90-45933
                                                                            CIP

The paper used in this publication is recycled and meets the
minimum requirements of American National Standard for
Information Sciences—Permanence of Paper for Printed Library
Materials, ANSI Z39.48-1984.

Unless otherwise indicated, Scripture quotations are from the
Holy Bible: New International Version. Copyright © 1973, 1978,
1984 International Bible Society. Used by permission of
Zondervan Bible Publishers.

Scripture quotations marked (KJV) are from the *King James
Version.*

The material in this book first appeared in *Christian Living.*

COUNTY ROAD 13
Copyright © 1990 by Herald Press, Scottdale, Pa. 15683
    Published simultaneously in Canada by Herald Press,
    Waterloo, Ont. N2L 6H7. All rights reserved.
Library of Congress Catalog Number: 90-45933
International Standard Book Number: 0-8361-3540-7
Printed in the United States of America
Cover art and book design by Merrill R. Miller

1 2 3 4 5 6 7 8 9 10 96 95 94 93 92 91 90

I dedicate this book to my wife, Anna Mae,

Who typed this manuscript
helped raise five children
permitted me to write
cheered me when depressed
sacrificed much
complained so little
during forty-three years of married life.

Thanks for loving the difficult to love.

Contents

Foreword

I first met Robert J. Baker at a mailbox along a rural route in Belleville, Pennsylvania. A high school freshman at the time, I was looking for ways to touch the world beyond the Kishacoquillas Valley.

Each week the *Youth's Christian Companion* offered contact with that world. I remember waiting beside the mailbox until the mailman's car drove up. Then, even before he had shifted gears to take off for the next drop, I was searching the pages for names like Esther Eby Glass, Edna Beiler, Paul Erb—and Robert J. Baker.

When I found the latter, I would stumble down the lane, oblivious to anything but the words on the page. Often I finished a Baker short story before I reached the house. What a world those stories opened! This writer spoke my language, talked about life in terms I could understand, put things together just right.

Twenty-five years later, as editor of *Christian Living* magazine, I needed a new columnist. I remembered Robert J. Baker. Would he continue to write about life in that everyday manner?

To my delight, he consented. He wasn't too enthusiastic, however, about "County Road 13," the title I thought up for his new column.

"But you're the editor," he said, after we had discussed it at length.

"You're the editor," he said, when we disagreed over whether he sent me purple passages or "merely ramblings" (as Bob confesses to in this book's preface). Usually we came to amiable agreement. I suspect, however, that some literary gems got lost in the editing process. Fortunately, Bob was never one to complain or hold offense.

For eleven years he has written—and continues to write—those columns. This book contains twenty-seven of them. They clearly show that the Baker wit and wisdom is as alive today as it was in 1954, when I first encountered it. Bob's reflections touch us all. Here is life as we know it if we're Bob's age—or life as we expect it, if we're younger.

Here are the fears of growing older: infirmities, surgeries, rejection, and ridicule from a society that values youth. Here are the joys of maturity: understanding, confidence, rest, and support from a caring church. Both are touched by the laughter of one who takes life seriously—but not too much so.

As he has done for more than twenty-five years, Bob allows us to see into both the ordinariness and transcendence of his world. In that glimpse, we see our own—and find new clarity and meaning in our own experience.

—J. Lorne Peachey
  Editor of Gospel Herald.

Author's Preface

When this book is published, I will be seventy. It's not a bad age, and I refuse to let society categorize me as obsolescent, a has-been. I am happy to be one of God's older production models. In the early 1900s the Creator put out some fine prototypes.

In 1979 I was asked to consider writing a column for the magazine *Christian Living*, put out by Mennonite Publishing House in Scottdale, Pennsylvania. The editor at the time was J. Lorne Peachey. He said, "What I am interested in is a column that would speak to the concerns of older adults: getting ready for retirement, living in retirement, health, finances, being useful, looking ahead." I accepted.

At that time I was fifty-nine, somewhat fearful of retirement and wondering if I could survive in the limbo between work and heaven. Nevertheless, in 1987, shortly before I turned sixty-seven, I retired and ended forty years of public school teaching.

Many of my fears never materialized. I am now a retirement veteran, having survived three years in this nebulous period of senior citizen discounts, Social Security checks, and such never-ending questions as "How do you like retirement? What are you doing during retirement? Since you are retired with nothing to do, would you mind mowing Aunt Matilda's lawn next Friday?"

I have written the columns once a month for the past ten years. In this book I will share twenty-seven columns that deal with the art of answering repetitive questions about retirement and informing those who believe you have passed on that you are still kicking.

We who are pushing extra digits still buy green bananas, expecting to be around to eat them. We do not necessarily retire to Florida or Arizona. We can still count to twenty. We do not live on prune juice and bran flakes. We would prefer that you not shout at us unless we ask you to speak up.

Growing older does not mean we lack opinions, are a menace on the highway, nap every day, go to sleep watching TV, and cannot teach a Sunday school class because we ramble too much. Long before I retired, I often took a nap. I have always rambled.

I am enjoying retirement. It is the greatest thing since sliced bread. You do not have to be old to enjoy this book. Many of my concerns are universal. But if you have been around a half century or so, I hope it will be a mirror, reflecting back to you many happy, as well as a few sad, images.

God is the oldest "person" I know. I think he is neat. I hope you will sense his loving hand on your shoulder as you read these sketches from my journey on County Road 13, Elkhart, Indiana.

I

Growing Older Is Normal

Today's world places a premium on youth. You don't see many old ladies with blue-tinted hair at reception desks, guarding the inner offices. "Young" goes nicely in front of "corporate executive." I have never seen a TV meteorologist or newscaster who came close to my three-score and ten.

I hear of face-lifts and all kinds of tucks that go from the belly on up. When we were kids, we couldn't wait to grow up; once we neared forty, we began backpedaling at top speed. The expression, "Thirty-nine and holding," came into vogue.

At the half-century mark, I gave up backpedaling. I no longer hand out quarters to those who underestimate my age. I don't stop speaking to those who overestimate. Of course, if they overshoot by five or so, I cross them off my Christmas list.

I snatch up each freebie offered to the senior citizen. I carelessly announce both age and birthday. I suggest well-wishers send money with their cards since I have all the neckties, back scratchers, and other gewgaws I need.

Growing older is normal. I am not one to stand in the way of progress. I follow the old maxim, "Every day, in every way, I'm getting better and better."

Why Fight It?

The advertisement ran frequently on the radio station. Every time I tuned in the news I also tuned in the solution to the ugly, brown spots appearing on my skin. The advertisement centered on an aging woman. She had just acquired a ring but refused to show it because those ugly, brown spots on her hand might give away her age.

Of course, there was a solution to the poor woman's problem. She had only to purchase a certain product, rub it on those nasties, and watch them fade, fade, fade. Ah, happiness.

I have also heard about the magic preparation one can gently rub into the skin to replace the natural oils lost with age. I look at my parched, checkered, and cracked hide. Should I invest in ten gallons for the tub and soak in it for a week?

Then there is the laser treatment you can try. The ad appeared in our local paper under the headline, "Look Years Younger!" A reporter interviewed the doctor performing the rejuvenation process. Twelve laser treatments cost only $600—as opposed to a surgical face-lift that might range from $3,500 to $7,000. So it's a bargain.

Facial muscles are stimulated by the class two or "cool" laser to contract as they did when one was young. The doctor says that 80 to 85 percent of the people undergoing the treatment have gained a three- to ten-year younger-looking appearance. The doctor offers a booster shot every six months but cautions, "You can't stop aging; you just push it back."

So I check myself in the mirror. Ah, the jowls definitely do sag. The face is lined with everything from those delicate crow's feet tracings near the eyes to the valleys and gulches in other areas where much larger animals have stomped and pawed. The face extends a frightful distance back. It trespasses over a scalp once covered by a heavy crop of hair but now eroded, fringed only with remnants and residues.

To make it even worse, at my last driver's license examination, the saucy young thing filling in the identification blanks checked me out. Then she said, loudly enough for all examiners and examinees to hear, "I think we better change this hair color from brown to gray." I gave a sickly nod and studied my nails. At least they grow nicely.

My friend dyes his hair and says it really helps. People look at the dark hair and say, "Hey, you've been losing weight, haven't you?" He chuckles at the way he fools the public with his act.

It's a fact. Drugstores are lined with bottles, jars, tubes, and packages containing rejuvenation oils, juices, hormones, vitamins, and minerals guaranteed to erase or retard the deterioration that comes with age. One does need to be careful. Invest in all of them at once, and you might pamper yourself back into diapers!

I should not make fun. It is only recently that I have been able to look at my antiqueness and see value in it. I well recall the sorrow I felt when my hair receded while I was still in college. For years, decades in fact, I wasted hours in artful combing to hide recession's progress. Finally I stopped. The task had become too great. Never did such a large area owe so much to so little.

The unfortunate thing is that our society places such a premium on youthful appearances that a person can feel ashamed of growing old. Yet, believe me, growing old is better than the alternative.

Please do not misunderstand me. I do not try to look older than threescore and ten. I neither flaunt my longevity nor despise it. I just accept it. If my clothes at times seem a bit sporty, it's because the grays, browns, and blacks are all gone by the time I hit the garage sale.

I do want to look respectable. The few hairs can be combed; they do not need to straggle in their isolation. The nails can be cleaned. Even brown spots on my face can be washed. A mouthwash never hurt anyone, regardless of years.

Ponce de Leon, a sixteenth-century Spanish explorer, spent years looking for the fountain of youth. Since he is no longer here, I presume he did not find it. It is only in heaven that we will never grow old.

I am often amused when I meet people for the

first time. Bad news travels fast, so perhaps they have heard the name before. They say to me (with undisguised sorrow, surprise, and sometimes even shock), "Somehow I pictured you differently."

Ah, yes, again, I am not six-foot-four, with piercing gray eyes that flash and sparkle from under a thick thatch of black hair (or iron gray, at least).

I tell them gently, "Sorry, I'm only five-foot-six, the eyes are a tired brown accented only by dark bags below, and the hair is a scarce gray."

They always quickly say, "No, no, that's not what I meant," but I march gaily ahead, splashing through their embarrassment to give a bit more of my gerontological philosophy:

"As I grow older, I care less and less what people think about me and more and more what God thinks of me. I expect to be with him much longer than with you.

"According to 1 Samuel 16:7, God looks at me differently. And I know that he accepts me, takes me with my glasses, bridgework, wrinkles, hair in full or scattered shocks, brown spots, and all that comes with growing older."

And that is what really matters.

Accusation at the Doggy Biscuit Barrel

When E. F. Hutton spoke, everyone supposedly listened. Remember those ads on TV where people stopped dead in their tracks, heads turned, ears perked, to hear a hot tip about the stock market?

Recently at a grocery store, a young lady of two or three fired an accusation at me. I suspect everyone within hearing range froze in their sneakers at her shrill cry. I did. Every grocery cart in the vicinity ground to a halt. Every customer and stock boy stood paralyzed. I had done nothing wrong. I was only quietly growing old as I sacked some dog biscuits from a barrel for a mixed poodle at home.

I had been in innocent conversation with the child's mother. The child, meanwhile, studied my wrinkled physiognomy. Finally she reached a verdict. With a loud cry from the grocery cart where she was strapped, she announced, "You are old!"

The child's piercing analysis was so unexpected, so out-of-the-blue, so blunt, so bold, it shocked every person at that end of the store. Never mind its accuracy. We just don't go around in public noting people's oldness. Not a cart moved, not a can was stocked. We were an E. F. Hutton ad.

I was bending over the barrel, sack half full, when I was labeled, identified, accused. I considered crawling into the barrel, yet I sensed people were waiting for a reaction.

Should I have pretended I was deaf? No, the mother already knew I was normal in that respect.

Should I have dropped the scoop and trod majestically to that wayward child? Should I have given her my sternest scowl, the one I reserved for teenage terrorists I taught in junior high? Without a word I could have had that snippet bawling.

Should I have said, with chilling clarity, "Madam, what kind of a child are you raising, who shows such cruel discrimination in public?"

Fortunately, I came to my senses. The child's analysis was correct—even if I did disapprove of her advertising it throughout the fresh fruits, dry cereals, and pet supplies department.

I retrieved myself from the barrel, gave the child a smile (somewhat forced), and said loudly so all could benefit, "That's right, little girl, I am old. Especially compared to you."

A collective sigh of relief seemed to rise from the northeast corner of the Family Leader Store. Grocery carts rolled again. The hum of voices resumed.

Then the mother entered the scene, saying, "Susan, that was not a nice thing to say." Translated, she meant, "Susan, it's bad enough to grow old without being reminded of it."

I said to the mother, "No, it's all right. We are all growing older. It's a normal thing."

I must confess I left the store a bit depressed. But as I drove home, I dreamed of an alternate scenario. I let my mind run wild; it took hilarious twists and I burst out laughing when it ended.

The scenario unraveled quickly as follows.

I could have said sadly to the child, to all the Hutton-like listeners, "Yes, little girl, I am old and poor. My wife and I have no dog. These biscuits are for us. Perhaps my wife will have a bit of jelly to put on them. They are so dry by themselves."

In my mind's dreaming, I see the mother take money from her purse. She says through tears, "You poor man. I insist you take this ten dollars."

Now my imagination is in high gear. I see other patrons coming forward, even the stock boys, raining money down upon me.

I get to the cash register. I am waved on by the manager, who says with a lump in his throat, "No charge, sir, no charge."

I walk slowly out of the store, carrying my dog biscuits, my pockets stuffed with numerous green bills. I have already decided to send all the cash to a charitable institution.

My woolgathering stopped as I drove into the garage. That's when I laughed aloud. Then sadness struck—I recalled hearing of poverty-stricken older people who have subsisted on pet food.

I told my wife the story. She agreed I handled it wisely. But when I shared my daydreaming, horror, followed by despair, crossed her face. "Bob," she said, "I don't see where you get your imagination."

I don't either. Is it the result of growing old?

II

Minor Surgery of Ancient Parts

We read of delicate brain surgery, of quadruple-bypass heart operations—and thrill to the wonders of modern medical science. But we would rather read about it than endure it.

When surgery comes to us, no matter how minor or commonplace, the shoe is slipped on the other foot. And even if the hospital trip is for nothing more than hernia repair, the idea of someone slicing intentionally through delicate tissue and invading your abdominal cavity is not my idea of adventure. I prefer to comfort others in pain, not squirm at my own.

With a master's degree in educational counseling, with a dozen years under my belt as a church elder, I supposedly have some skills in advising others. But the skills reach outward, not inward.

In these two chapters, come laugh at me and with me, as I submit to minor blood-letting with great reluctance. I find it ten times funnier now than I did back then.

Anticipating the Knife

My wife had made her cryptic notes on the calendar in the kitchen, the calendar that was to remind us of dates we dared not miss. For April 15, 1986, she had simply marked, "Pre-op." I presumed that was pre-operation. For April 17, two days later, the calendar read, "Hernia op." For any dummy, that translated, "Hernia operation."

I'd been watching the date approach with little anticipation. The temptation was to call the surgeon and say, "Scrub the scrubbing: I've changed my mind." The old term we used for that was "chickening out."

During World War II, I was the only medic aboard the LCT 534, a landing craft tank ship. We took tanks into Utah Beach, France, and evacuated wounded to the hospital ship offshore. The wounded were broken, sliced, punctured, torn. Many were in deep pain. I moved among them, examining their wound tags, checking for the last morphine shot, giving water when possible. I adjusted bandages, loosened a tourniquet, gently squeezed a shoulder.

Now, under much more aseptic conditions, I

awaited a small wound. I watched the calendar roll around. I was ashamed of my apprehension. I always glibly recommended the stiff upper lip.

But that was when it was them. Now it was me. And although mine was *pianissimo* surgery, I dreaded this dinky trip to the hospital. My macho image had sprung a leak.

My first warning that I was falling apart came on the tennis court. A summer ago, as I scrambled around, I had the funny sensation that something inside the old lower body cavity was swinging freely. Strange, but no sweat. Perhaps everyone as they aged developed these little internal pendulums.

I tossed it off as insignificant, especially since it did not throw off my tennis game. I was consistently beating my daughter. I just let the abdominal swinging swing.

The swinging stopped as miraculously as it had appeared, good for only one summer. Then a new symptom or two. A slight bulge. Sometimes a stinging near the bulge. Stomach gurgles from the lower left quadrant of the abdomen.

I thought I knew the answer: hernia. For $20 my physician confirmed this. (The word *hernia* comes from the Greek and means "offshoot." In my case, a loop of bowel was sticking out through a weak spot in the muscular wall of the abdomen.)

I was referred to an M.D. who specialized in correcting these problems. For another $20, he confirmed the first doctor's diagnosis. This surgeon was a laid-back one. No hurry—but the operation ought to be completed sometime.

With a twinkle in his eye, he said, "If the hernia strangulates, gets choked off, you have about eight hours before gangrene sets in. You should be able to get to a hospital in time."

My eyes did not twinkle back. To calm me, he described how no general anesthetic was used. I would be perfectly conscious during the surgery.

I went home, deciding to wait it out a few years. After all, it was not interfering with my tennis game. Besides, hernias, for some strange reason, are not glamorous. Best keep it quiet.

But the stinging got worse. It began to appear periodically the last hour of the teaching day. I wanted to blame it on my eighth-hour class, a class full of pistols, all loaded.

My wife said, "The present school insurance is good, Medicare is a backup, you have over a hundred sick-leave days, why fool around?" Of course, it was my hernia. But she was right. So I called.

The seventeenth came on a Thursday. I was to be home Thursday through Sunday. The doctor had briefed me on how hernias were done now. He even showed me a video.

Evidently he followed a set recipe. "No general anesthetic. Come in at 6:00 a.m. We will have you home by 10:30 a.m. Outpatient only. You will be conscious during the operation, nothing to worry about. Four days of recuperation will do it. Just take it easy when you go back."

He went on to tell me about the Amish patient he repaired who pushed too hard and tore out his sutures while carrying filled milk cans. The surgeon added, with (I thought) a bit of pride, "My threads held, but not the tissue."

Well, I wouldn't be carrying more than a brief-case. No milk cans for me. The surgeon did have a bit of humor about him, not stuffy. But the idea of lying there awake while they opened me up did not set me dancing for joy.

The assistant principal of our school had had the same operation a month before. He was my age and survived. He mentioned the various shots they gave to make him groggy. And the fact that if things got touchy during the cutting, the medics were willing to give a bit more local anesthetic. He said the only pain he felt during the ensuing weeks was when he sat down or got up. None of this excited me.

I realized that I was majoring in minors; a bit of pain, some inconvenience, some expense. It was a little shocking to me. I had had sixty-five years of good health. Now several failures were cropping up. I was reminded of Oliver Wendell Holmes' poem "The Deacon's Masterpiece," an account of the construction of a superb one-hoss shay, which completely collapsed after one hundred years of good use.

> You see, of course, if you're not a dunce,
> How it went to pieces all at once.

I think the Lord was humbling me, teaching me. Words of advice, chickens I had glibly scattered about, like "Just trust in the Lord. Everything will work out. A little pain never hurt anyone," were coming home to roost. I heard again the sermon I so easily preached from Ephesians 5:20 (NIV), "Always giving thanks to God the Father for everything."

Okay, Lord, thanks for April 17, 1986, but excuse me if once in awhile I preface or conclude my thanks with an "Ouch!"

Major Suffering from Minor Surgery

We were in the holding room of the Elkhart (Ind.) General Hospital, stretched out on our beds in two neat rows. Nurses and orderlies buzzed around and occasionally a doctor stepped in. I was waiting for the shot in my gluteus maximus muscle to take effect. Despite the minor discomfort, things seemed to be in sharp focus in the dimly lit room.

On my right, the intravenous bottle dripped monotonously. Its contents slipped down the clear plastic tube, through the needle, into my vein.

To my left, my neighbor also awaited removal to the operating room. She was loquacious. She was old, older even than I, and more experienced at hospital procedures. She had had three operations in one year—this trip was for gallstones.

When I told her that I was in for a hernia repair, she snorted, "I had a hernia operation over a year ago, and that spot hasn't felt right since!"

I hardly needed such testimony. This was my first trip to the operating room. I did not need organ recitals by others to remind me of what I was about to experience.

I halfheartedly said to my disconsolate friend, "Maybe I'll get up and walk out."

She snickered, "You would look funny trying to walk out of here in your little nightie. . . ." I tried to smile, to relax under the sheet and blanket.

As I overheard snatches of conversation from nurses, doctors, orderlies, and patients, I realized my little old hernia was at the bottom of the totem pole in seriousness. No one dies from hernia repair. (I felt like apologizing for taking up space.) But would I prefer to raise my status with triple-by-pass heart surgery or a delicate brain exploration? No thanks! I'd take the lowly hernia.

The orderly came. Everyone kept asking me my name. Good—I didn't care to lose something I needed. In the operating room, I was strapped to the narrow table under bright lights. The nurse explained this was because the table was narrow. I suspect they were concerned I would try to walk out.

Before they wheeled me to the holding room, I said to my wife, "I'm not looking forward to this."

"I'll be seeing you," she said.

Two doctors and two nurses surrounded me—escape was impossible. I was scrubbed with an ice-cold liquid that only increased the tension of my drum-tight abdomen. More anesthetic was given, all local.

There was jolly conversation among the medical staff. They discussed vacations, other doctors, eating out, and future plans. I lay there hoping I was not taking up too much of their valuable time.

Occasionally, the friendly surgeon threw a word my way: "Try to relax." Or, "Let me know if you feel any pain."

As they progressed, I awkwardly raised my head, the only part of me that had any freedom. I wanted to check out what they were doing with the hemostats and retractors.

The surgeon sliced through the various layers of tissue to reach the spot where the intestine had bulged out of the abdominal wall. He complained good-naturedly about my wife's cooking, commenting that the fat was giving him some trouble.

I heard him say, with what I interpreted as concern, "This is very thin."

The assisting surgeon muttered something I couldn't catch. I verbalized my own concern at their concern.

The surgeon simply continued his attack, saying to me, "Don't worry, unless you hear me say 'Oops!'"

I dropped my head back. Better to have a happy surgeon than one venting unhappiness on my insides.

I was amazed at the total lack of pain. And I was curious—but the view was not the best. By doing periodic sit-ups with just my head, I could get a slanting view of the action. From time to time, the surgeon would point out something of interest to the medical spectators.

Once when my head was raised, a bit of tugging enabled him to show me a tiny white tube. He said, "Here's your *vas deferens*." I dropped my head back with a thud. I didn't want my curiosity to cause them to go out of their way on the tour. I'd take the psalmist's word for it. "I am fearfully and wonderfully made" (Psalm 139:14, KJV).

Finally, the intestine was tucked back into its proper slot, the escape hole closed. The tissues were patted back into place and sutured. An oversized Band-Aid was slapped on. Then I went back to my wife, to whom the surgeon gave instructions. Evidently he did not trust me.

At home I was waited on hand and foot. Everything was lovely until about noon. By then the anesthetic had worn off, and I began to feel the pain. A generic painkiller, my only solace, helped alleviate the sharpness of the pain when I sat or lay still. Nothing helped if I bent, which I had to do to sit down or stand up. I hurt. I wished the doctor had given me something stronger for my pain.

Two mornings after the operation, I was reading from Job. Eliphaz the Temanite had words for me:

> Think how you have instructed many,
>   how you have strengthened feeble hands.
> Your words have supported those who stumbled;
>   you have strengthened faltering knees.
> But now trouble comes to you, and you are
>   discouraged;
>   it strikes you, and you are dismayed.
>   (Job 4:3-5, NIV)

How true. I was ashamed. To sleep on my back for a few weeks, to wince when I sat down and stood up was not the end of the world. I was in a world where there was much more intense suffering. But my slight taste of pain at least placed me in a better position to visit, to reach out to the suffering and hurting.

Probably my hernia came because of trying to lift too much, stretch too far. My own clumsiness had hurt me. A spiritual hernia would be something to shout about—hurting myself because I stretched too far, lifted too much, trying to help others.

III

Moaning and Groaning

Most of us are defensive. And usually we defend our own and present turf. We have arguments to support our politics, the athletic teams we cheer, the newsmagazines to which we subscribe. Unfortunately, at times we become blind to other political parties, sports teams, newsmagazines. Many times our choices are lifelong ones. Frankly, I have long leaned toward the Republican Party, split my limited cheering between Indiana and Notre Dame universities, and read Newsweek. But in relation to life stages, I've been a "changer."

Once I thought being a teenager was the cat's meow. Later the young marrieds took first place, only to be superseded by stable middle-agers. Today, I champion the mature folk. So I'm fickle.

Some of my gripes and groans are tongue in cheek. Some arise from righteous indignation. Society is mostly kind to us mature ones, but I dislike discrimination, being coddled, being labeled. In this section, and in others to some extent, I revel in the great American sport—complaining. It's a privilege that comes with age.

Actually each stage of life can be the best. I like where I am at, so please don't knock it.

Identifying "Old People"

I suppose he was twenty-five years my junior, perhaps thirty. And he addressed me as "young man." I gritted my teeth. But he was a skilled physician, caring most competently for a loved one. I thought, *Again, I turn the other cheek.* I expected the acquaintanceship to be brief; it was.

Now why did his "young man" business grind me? After all, was it not better than "old man"? Not much. They both accomplish the same purpose.

To me they seem like ways of saying, "Well, Mr. Baker, you've been hanging around a long time. I'll stroke you a mite with this bit of flattery, brighten your twilight years, see if I can put a sparkle in those ancient eyes.

"Everyone can tell you are about ready for the glue factory. But let's try and ignore it. We'll pretend you're a young blade of twenty-one."

That's what I call "reverse psychology" name calling. It also happens when we call large people "Tiny" or "Slim" and slap the label "Curly" on a bald man. Such name tags are only slightly more flattering than "Fatty" or "Baldy."

Why do we do it? It's simply another way the user calls attention to what he considers a fault, a defect, an oddity in others. It's a way of lording it over another, of saying, "Lord, I thank you that I am not as others are—fat, bald, or old. I am not overweight, I have all my hair, and I am in the prime of time" (Luke 18:11-12, Bakersonian Translation).

We who have survived the years get used to this, for we face some interesting nomenclature. We are said to be "senior citizens." This, I presume, means we are about ready to graduate.

We are noted for being in our "sunset years." This must mean day is dying in the west, and it's time to go to our rooms, pull down the shade, crawl into bed, assume a fetal position, pull the sheet over the head, and quietly sink below the horizon.

Upon occasion we are identified as those in our "golden years." Why golden? Is such a description a propaganda ploy to keep me quiet, like sticking a pacifier in a squealing baby's mouth? The last years for many older people in this world are not golden, for gold does not tarnish. They may be golden for me. But such mass labeling seems inappropriate when applied to the aged living on a steam grate in New York City weather or lying, unvisited, in a nursing home.

On occasions, we are simply dumped into the "retiree" basket. This is usually labeled "out," not "in." Even the home church has tagged us. We are assigned to the "grandpa-grandma" Sunday school class—but supplied with no candy peppermints. Sometimes, even more crudely, we are simply classed as "old crocks." I wonder if they think of me as being an empty five-gallon crock that formerly held sauerkraut?

For some we are the "ancients of days," the "sixty-fivers," the "oldies." Well, in forty years of school teaching, I was called worse.

Sorry if I am beginning to sound like a sorehead. But I don't want to be coddled, amused, pampered until I am ready for Pampers. Being old does not depersonalize me.

By now some readers are bewildered. You are dismayed at my paranoia, my sensitivity. You say, "But what shall I call . . . you 'older' people . . . I mean, you more 'mature' ones. . . . Oh, I don't know what I mean!"

Relax. Remember several things, and then hang loose.

First, when you label a person, you say something about the classifier as well as the one classified. Each "labeler" will have to analyze his or motivation in choosing labels. It is a complex situation. And unfortunately, geriatric psychology is a "Johnny-come-lately" affair.

Second, remember this: anytime we classify a person, whether young or old, we run the danger of losing that person as an individual. The person becomes a statistic, a percentage, a number in the third column of Table V, p. 316, see Appendix B.

No grouping or labeling is perfect, uniform, inclusive. Within the grouping are subgroupings, subclasses. And finally, within that smallest section are the individuals. When you classify us mature ones, don't lose me. Let me have identity.

Third, remember that any age is a good age to be at, if God is there. Sixty is no exception. So the next time you see me or another plus sexagenarian (I refer to our age, not our morality), see us as a brother, a sister in Christ, a kindred soul, fairly normal. "Brother Bob," or "Brother Baker" is always in order. In fact, I consider it downright brotherly.

As I grow older, I still expect to remain human, to be a part of the family of God. I will grow older; nothing can stop it. But please don't push it, accelerate it. Don't saddle me with names that suggest I am riding down the last lonely trail, the final sands are trickling through my particular hourglass, this ship is on its final voyage and tenderly approaches final harbor. I know I will never be eighteen again—you don't need to sing it to me.

Let me live as an individual. Don't bulk mail me like I was going to a bunch of "occupant" homes. Let me be myself.

Let me think of myself as a person of worth, not one twice over the hill, stumbling to his final, heavenly home, only reading the Bible because I am cramming for my final exam. Who knows? Perhaps God will want me, at seventy, to try my wings again and fly higher than I ever flew before.

Sticks and Stones

For me the expression goes back a half century. When quarreling with neighborhood children who used name-calling with great skill, we often chanted back, "Sticks and stones may break my bones, but words can never hurt me."

For some strange reason, we attributed the saying to Shakespeare. Stevenson's rather exhaustive tome, *Home Book of Quotations*, does not even list our trite little rebuttal. So it must have been our midsummer night's dream, not Shakespeare's.

Regardless, the statement is not true. To say that words do not hurt us means we are either saints or liars, most likely the latter. True, we may bear up bravely, brush the invectives off, and shrug the calloused shoulders. But the cutting words excise with pain; the wounded flesh heals slowly.

Leviticus 19:32 reads so nicely: "Thou shalt rise up before the hoary [gray] head, and honor the face of the old man, and fear thy God: I am the Lord"(KJV). But believe me, it is not always done.

Now I am not bitter, but neither would I deny the obvious. Let me give three examples of when I felt the sharp slap, basically because of my age.

There was this sale on men's dress slacks at the local clothing store. Eager for a bargain, I was met in the store by a downy-cheeked clerk who inquired if he could help. Eagerly I mentioned the advertised slacks.

I can still see his look of sadness, bordering on pity, as he said with sorrow, "Oh, I am so sorry, but those on sale are all young men's styles."

I stopped, petrified, silenced, shamed. Here I was, evidently a decrepit dinosaur, trying to act and camouflage myself as a graceful gazelle. How disgraceful.

Without a word, I turned and left, tail between my legs, but too ashamed to even whimper. Although I did not literally shake the dust off my feet, I never returned to that store again. To my chagrin, they are still in business, prospering in spite of my stout boycott.

I was deeply involved in planning a new program at our school for gifted children. It was my privilege to describe the course and introduce the young teacher of the science part of the program to a large group of parents. After the meeting I stood beside the young teacher, ready to help him answer questions from doting mothers and fathers.

The first mother rushed up to him, gushed over him, and said, enraptured, "Oh, I am so glad they selected a young male teacher for this position."

I had a little trouble breathing and moved to a part of the room where the air was less strangling. The mother continued to bubble and exude. I alternately boiled and sniveled, trying to restrain my hopes that her son would bungle the course.

That school year is long over, and Sam (not his real name) is history. He gave me a bad time for 178 days of the 180-day school year (unfortunately, he was absent only twice).

At the first parent-teacher meeting, I cornered his father and inquired as to the possible cause of Sam's antagonism. Sam's father looked at me with cold, cold eyes and said, "I don't know, except Sam says he just doesn't like old people."

I explained to Sam's father that there wasn't a good deal I could do about that. The father, sprawled on a chair as he waited for an interview with another teacher, simply shrugged his shoulders. Meeting the father did help me suffer through that year with Sam; heredity is pretty powerful stuff.

Our "Shakespeare" was wrong—words hurt. James was more correct: "The tongue also is a fire. . . . No man can tame the tongue" (James 3:6, 8, NIV). I doubt if the store clerk, the mother of the gifted child, even Sam, would literally kick an elderly person (well, maybe Sam would). But they kicked me with words, demeaning words that suggested one is automatically disqualified for certain things as one ages. If I did not know better, by now the hydrochloric acid in my stomach would have multiplied so that even Rolaids could not have absorbed and neutralized it.

But I am reminded of Bob Gallager. The Lord brought him to mind as I pondered my earlier years, wondering if I had ever been disrespectful to my elders. In the first survey, I came through pure as snow. Then the Lord reminded me of Bob Gallager. And I was shamed.

Bob Gallager was a recluse, a ragpicker, a junk man. He went about Elkhart pushing an old two-wheeled cart through the alleys, gleaning odds and ends to sell. And boys like me, boys who should have known better, would holler at him:

"Old Bob Gallager,
Sitting on a fence,
Trying to make a dollar
Out of fifteen cents."

Our ridicule would enrage him and please us. I write with shame. Bob Gallager is dead, so I cannot go to him and ask forgiveness. But I have gone to God and found forgiveness there.

Why share my Bob Gallager story with others? Penitence, I guess. Besides, store clerks, mothers of gifted children, and several "Sams" somehow do not seem so obnoxious, so thoughtless, or so cruel when I review and find that my own stance in the past was imperfect.

Strange—as you grow older you become wiser, more tolerant, understanding, forgiving, sensitive, introspective. Like so many things, one improves with age.

Old but Not Stupid

As the oldest teacher among some fifty professionals in our school building, I was often the recipient of sly little comments about "senility." They came good-naturedly, and because I remembered my own tongue can be sharp as a serpent, I usually shrugged them off in like manner.

Besides, I believe I know something of my mental ability. I think I do fairly well for being a "dinosaur." After all, I am not yet extinct. The old adage, "There's no fool like an old fool," applies to romancing, not thinking.

While teaching, I was asked to help handle the United Way campaign at our school. One day as I was urging a clump of teachers in the hallway to make a pledge, one of the younger squirts said, "Now, Baker, you know the only reason you are pushing this is because of the benefits you expect to receive from old age assistance." His comment drew several snickers.

I like to think the Lord, not my sharp tongue, gave me the ready answer. Focusing my sixty-year-old eyes on his of a mere thirty, I said, "Well, it's not just the elderly that United Way helps; it's also the mentally handicapped."

The laughs outdrew the snickers. I do believe in turning the other cheek. But on occasion, a sharp retort is needed to help my brother sublimate his sneer into something more sublime. When it comes to hints at senility, that's the time to use it.

My American College Dictionary says of *senile*: "Pertaining to, or characteristic of old age." Of *senility* it says: "The weakness or mental infirmity of old age." How nice of them to lump all of us mature ones into such a simplistic bag!

I know little about writing a dictionary, but as a science teacher I learned something about the human brain, the last frontier. And I find it fabulous. So much of our response to stimuli is automatic that most of us take this wonder for granted. Regardless of my IQ, every day I should thank God for my brain. Just to be average is beautiful.

Weighing only about three pounds, using no more energy than a 75-watt light bulb, this complex structure of the brain may be screening as many as one hundred million tidbits of sensory information per second (that's no misprint). Fortunately, most of these stimuli are filtered out, rejected, discarded. Otherwise, one might be in an almost constant state of "seizure," as electrical storm after electrical storm raced through the brain.

Someone has suggested that a computer large enough to duplicate the functioning of a single brain would cover the face of the entire earth. Skilled and learned psychologists, psychiatrists, and neurosurgeons pry, poke, and probe at the brain. They try to force that miraculous organ to give up its secrets.

How does the brain receive and store information, process data, creatively plan? Why does it sometimes self-destruct and leave the body helpless? We question, but what we have learned is surely outweighed by knowledge yet to come.

I have read estimates of neurons (nerve cells) in our brain that run all the way from ten billion to thirty billion, with perhaps five billion in the cortex of the brain alone.

But there's another side. By middle age those neurons are dying off at the rate of one hundred thousand per day. They are not replaceable. Even as you read this short paragraph, several hundred became mental sawdust and went down the tube. Perhaps the constant flaking away of neuron cells is why they describe some people as "pretty flaky."

Does such deterioration mean we mature ones are undone, a people of diminishing neurons? Does stupidity stare us in the face? Are the senility forecasters right?

Suppose the old powerhouse has shrunk by 10 percent when we hit seventy. Does that mean we are on the skids to the convalescent home, there to become rheumy-eyed and palsy-handed, our Jello treat at 8:00 p.m. the highlight of the day?

Nonsense! Rubbish! Garbage!

Senility may come but not because we have lost a few neurons. It is estimated that most people use under 10 percent of their brainpower during their lifetime. There is plenty left to draw on as we age.

In addition, we have sixty or seventy years of experience up there that is unmatched by a twenty- or thirty-year old brain that isn't even broken in yet. The gracious Lord has given us enough neurons so that even if we do lose one hundred thousand per day, there is sufficient supply to last at least four hundred years. By that time I expect to have traded in the old model for one carrying a guarantee for all of eternity.

We whom God has blessed with years may need to work a bit harder with what we have. But with balanced diets, reasonable blood pressure, exercise, sufficient sleep, and positive thinking, there is no reason for us to be branded senile.

I do not deny there is such a thing as senility. But I deny vigorously that old age equals senility. Clearly there are physical factors that can slow down thought processes. But they are not limited only to people of mature age.

Every night when I retire, I like to recall the day—the pluses, the minuses. And when I do, I always end up with something like this for a prayer:

"Lord, today I made some mistakes with the old computer upstairs. It didn't misfire; I punched the wrong keys. You didn't make me a robot; you gave me a mind. It's average, Lord, but I praise you for it. Help me program it for tomorrow.

"Refresh me now with sleep. Slow those mental circuits. Then tomorrow throw the whole works into overdrive for you.

"Good-night, Lord."

IV

My Retirement Diary

After some years of retirement, I look back with amusement at what I wrote earlier. I smile at my fears, defenses, and schemes to get people off my back, both before and after retirement. Writers often have vivid imaginations and exaggerate. Take my complaints and solutions with a large grain of salt. My wife says I have a martyr's complex—and she is usually right about me.

Let me say, before you read my retirement growlings, that God and I have always had a good relationship. God has kept working with me, even after I retired. I now have time to better know him.

Preparing for and entering retirement is bound to cause fear and trepidation. But it is also fun, exciting, a stimulating journey into the unknown. I always wanted to be an explorer.

I have chosen four snapshots dealing with my retirement. They form sort of a retirement diary. Come frown with me, be puzzled—and smile.

I am happy for those of you approaching or already on this retirement odyssey. Beautiful. And may the wind be always at your back.

Check List for the Nosy (1986)

I've been thinking of having this little card printed. It would contain my name and the statement, "In reference to your question, 'When are you going to retire?' please note the checklist below." Underneath I would have a number of choices I would quickly scan through. According to how I felt that day and who the questioner was, I would check the right answer, hand the card to the inquisitive one, and tip my hat. Then I would be merrily on my way, seeking to answer some of life's weightier questions.

And what choices might I check in reference to my retirement date? They might run like this:

—I consider my retirement date a personal matter. Thanks for not inquiring further.

—Why do you ask? Do you want my job? If so, take a number, but start praying you can find other work.

—It all depends upon my financial situation. If you give me, not loan me, $50,000 immediately, I will take a chance on retirement today.

—You should be glad that I am still working and

contributing to Social Security instead of sub-
tracting from it. Keep bugging me, and I will
quit, increasing your own tax burden.

—The Lord hasn't told me yet and I'm surprised
that he is talking to you about our business.

—Why do you ask? I am only sixty-five and Caleb
knocked off the Hebronites when he was eighty-
five. Check me out again, around 2005, if you are
still around.

Now, I know that printing and using such a card
would not win me many friends. And it might
cause more people to question my mental equilibri-
um. Yet the checklist card is becoming ever more
attractive to me.

Never a week goes by without someone dropping
the hammer on my head, saying, "Well, when do
you plan to retire?"

The question seems to be coming with greater
frequency. I suppose this is par for the course, normal for wrinkled, tottery ones with white-fringed
heads. Maybe I am getting paranoid on the subject.
Am I not still competent? Can't I still add, subtract,
read the comics, answer the telephone, turn on the
television? Can't I still do all those little things that
people seem to consider essential to life, liberty,
and the pursuit of happiness?

Are the older ones who question me looking for
a new convert to their ranks? Are the younger ones
jealous that I can call it quits whenever I choose? Is
the question born of admiration or pity?

Sorry if I sound like one who receives junk mail
that begins "Congratulations! You have been select-

ed to receive . . ." but I am a wee bit suspicious about all the inquiries indicating I should know what I do not know.

God has only indicated, "You can't go on forever." He has never said, poetlike, "I'm calling you to heaven, so quit before you are sixty-seven."

True, the Elkhart Community School Board recently laid down the law for all of us oldies, telling us politely that after one is seventy there is nothing left in the cranium for distribution. It is kind of them to date so specifically the time of my mental deterioration. But even then, I could still teach until the summer of 1991, if I so choose, which I probably won't.

Of course, I have exaggerated my reaction a bit, becoming a mite splenetic, peevish, perhaps even somewhat vitriolic. As you grow older, your two leading and evolving characteristics are sarcasm and the frantic search for big words to use, so people will not think you have slipped back into childhood memories of "Run, Spot, run."

People seem either to have decided or are determined to set up a date for me to end it all, wrap up my teaching, retire. The other Sunday evening, at church, we had a number of visitors. One yuppie, whom I have not seen for several years, sat down beside me, slapped me on the knee, and said, "So this is your last year of teaching?"

I answered, "Oh, is it? I hadn't heard." I had a notion to add, "You know they can't fire me unless they prove I am incompetent, immoral, or insubordinate. Which of the three am I guilty of?" My friend quickly backed off.

I may be "mountainizing" a molehill, but retirement involves many details to be worked out, problems to be solved. There is more involved than my simply snapping out a date for the wondering one who says, "When are you retiring?"

Please don't ask me that question unless you are prepared to sit down with me and discuss the things yet hanging fire—matters of insurance, savings, Social Security, state pensions, severance pay, letter of resignation, taxes, debts, IRAs, tax-sheltered annuities, school responsibilities, church responsibilities, Internal Revenue Service, and so on.

My wife and I are dealing with those items, plus a few more. That seems normal to me. We got married together, and it seems we should retire together. After forty years of marriage (minus one), five children, seven grandchildren (four in the same year), we should be able to work out my retirement between us. If we have questions about it, let us ask them. Don't call us, we'll call you.

Anyway, it's not a life-or-death matter. Retirement or continuing to work are not the opposite ends of some morality line—one end right, the other wrong. I don't think we will be sinning, whatever we decide.

Frankly, I don't know when I am going to retire, and I seriously doubt if most of the inquirers give two hoots one way or another. But to be on the safe side of it, I will add one more selection to the others outlined above.

—Thanks for your interest. I can discuss this better over a dinner date. Please call to make an appointment. We prefer expensive restaurants.

The way I look at it, God has the future pretty well locked up. I would be surprised if one of these days he didn't clue us in on when I should retire. Meanwhile, I do wish people would sit tight until I get my checklist printed.

Slipping Out Quietly (1987)

During the past five years, the manila file folder labeled "Retirement" has grown fatter. The handwriting was on the wall. I would be sixty-five just after school started in the fall of 1985. That meant my teaching career would end in June of 1986.

Then the handwriting was erased by the raising of the mandatory retirement age to seventy, adding five years of grace. Wow! I could go until 1991. There was one catch—in June of 1991, I would be 70.75 years old. I would have spent forty-four years in the teaching arena. Too long!

There have been changes in that classroom, too many for this old codger. Like Frank Buck, animal trainer of the past, I found myself cracking the whip too frequently. I was firing the blank pistol too often as I tried to get the snarling charges to perform. It was getting to be a circus, and too often I left the school feeling the tigers had won. When I began wondering if teachers should be issued live ammunition instead of blanks, I knew it was time to pack it in and pick a finishing spot. And it would have to be before 1991.

My good wife and I talked about it for the past several years. Graciously, she did not pressure me either way. But I sensed a gentle leading from her toward my calling it quits long before the 1991 date.

So we added another paper to the retirement folder. It is dated August 27, 1986, addressed to the personnel director of the Elkhart Community Schools. The first paragraph of that letter said, "After considerable soul-searching, I believe this should be my last year of teaching service."

It has been a struggle, determining a retirement date. I am now locked into it, the die is cast, the Rubicon crossed. June 4, 1987, is just two months down the road from typing this on April 4, 1987, a bit past April Fools' Day. And my thoughts are winging, swirling. What will it be like—retirement?

Although Anna Mae and I agree on the retirement time, we have disagreed on the public announcement of it. I have attempted to mask it, hide it as long as possible.

Anna Mae says, "Why keep it a secret?" She is puzzled by my past insistence that it be kept quiet. In my resignation letter, I asked for no publicity. I made my principal pledge that he would make no official announcement to the local faculty.

When asked by students how long I would be teaching, I quipped back, "I have never believed in evolution. But I thought I would give it one more chance. I'll wait and teach your children to see if there is any improvement."

Once a teaching nemesis of mine loudly asked at

a faculty meeting, "When is Baker going to retire?"

I snapped back, "I'll stop teaching when you begin." Our banter drew laughter but was a cover-up on my part.

But in a few months, the cat will be fully out of the bag. The local paper will have printed the list of retirees for this year, my name included. The retirement dinner will have taken place. The faculty at my school will have given me a gift certificate, a fishing rod, or perhaps a new coffeepot in honor of the countless cups I have consumed on the school premises.

Why have I been so reluctant to publicize my retirement, even though it was fixed back there in August? It is now leaking out and soon will of necessity become public knowledge.

Perhaps it has been a last ditch effort of the subconscious to deny what is happening. Stupid, but a possibility. I have done dumber things. Climactic events are always happening to others, never to us. Others grow old while we bathe eternally in fountains of youth.

Perhaps pupil-teacher relationships have been one legitimate reason for my quietness. I have seen some teachers taken advantage of because their role was ending. Like with a substitute, some pupils will always take advantage of what they feel is a weakness, a lack of permanence in the establishment. Why should I invite trouble?

Or what if perchance the opposite should occur, my retirement generating mass sympathy from pupils for the old geezer? Well, I do not need that, either. I prefer to stand on my own two feet until the end.

Perhaps I should confess my sense that work brings status. When questioned about my vocation, I have always said with some satisfaction, "I am a school teacher." I have accepted both the pleased looks and the gasps of horror. I have accepted the twice-monthly payments for services rendered with a feeling that I have earned them.

On retirement, do I become a *persona non grata*, not acceptable, not wanted? True, I have other spheres of activity, but teaching was the biggie. It was the one that brought in the shekels, the prestige. Will I become a nonentity? Do I need to rediscover who I actually am?

I will be drawing a new variety of checks. One from Social Security, another from the Indiana State Teachers Retirement Fund—for doing not one lick of work. To an accused workaholic, that sounds like treason. It seems strange (to say the least), shameful (at the most).

In spite of those who say, "You deserve it," or "You have suffered enough," or "Everyone else does it," I wonder. In response I ask, "Do I?" "Have I?" "Should I?"

One more reason for my reluctance. Is retirement a sign of weakness? By it, do I say, "I've had it"? Does it look to others like a sign of weakness, surrender in the midst of the battle? Perhaps I should have waited until they carried me out on a stretcher, weakly waving a piece of chalk.

Tomorrow, God willing, I will tell my church

cluster about our decision. From there it will leak out to the rest of the church family. Those who don't sniff out the news from them will read it here. Those who don't read this don't deserve to know—and probably could not care less.

I suppose this chapter is sad. The writer seems ashamed of what he has done. He must be a diehard, a stubborn old goat who is now crying in his decaffeinated cup, his weak tea.

Not so! I am just new at retiring. It's like going to school, getting married, facing your first classroom, dying. You have to do those things for the first time to really test them out.

I've tried the first two, university and marriage. Neither was too bad. Without asking Anna Mae's opinion, I think I have succeeded in both university and marriage, give or take a few low grades in both. Now I propose to take a crack at retirement. I have put off dying to a later date, haven't even started a manila file folder on it yet.

I expect to pick up some firsthand experience on retirement in the next twenty or so years. I am fast filing papers for Social Security, teacher pension benefits, supplements to Medicare insurance.

I checked things out with God the other day, looking for a little counsel about this retirement phase of life. He confessed he had no experience in retirement. I found this confession comforting. It makes mine easier. It looks like God was around when I went to the university, got married, and will still be holding my hand in retirement and the last big adventure, dying. I figure on surviving them both.

Retirement: Year One (1988)

"How does it feel to be retired?"

Since June 4, 1987, that is a question I've been asked again and again. I am still looking for a sharp answer. So far, none has arisen. I am surprised that people query me about a subject concerning which I know so little. I have barely stuck my toes in the water to test the temperature, yet people act as if I have already swum the English channel.

Admittedly, I am sometimes alarmed at my own reaction to the question. Has retirement suddenly made me more cantankerous, irritable, snappish? But then I realize I have always preferred to hand out my own news releases, on a schedule preferably determined by myself, and only after due preparation.

When I am forced to do business with the questions, I have considered breaking into crocodile tears. I have debated throwing myself on the questioner, sobbing about my unfortunate lot as I spin in the whirlpool of society's rejects, and asking if I might be lent $500 to pay taxes and save the old homestead. It would be interesting to watch the reaction.

Or I could take the opposite approach. I could tell how retirement is the greatest thing since sliced bread, gush over the size of my pension and Social Security checks, tell them we are thinking of a trip around the world to celebrate—and watch the green of envy emerge.

Then I'd chastise my questioners for breaking the tenth commandment concerning coveting. I would write their pastor a note about their sin. But that would be entrapment, legally and morally unacceptable.

Maybe I should be less critical of those who inquire. People mean well, perhaps genuinely worry about me. I think some pity me, wonder if I can shift down in my life's pattern without stripping my mental transmission.

But how can I explain about retirement when I have not yet experienced it to any degree? They might as well ask me about my experience on Wall Street, my adventures as president of the U.S., my life as an astronaut, the joys and sorrows of robbing banks. I have had no experience in any. The question is out of sequence.

I have read about retirement. We've done some planning for it. And I expect the coming years to reveal the truth of what I have read and reveal the strengths and weaknesses of our planning.

I do not expect to issue daily communiques of progress or regression. Retirement surely is not as volatile as the stock market. Furthermore, I feel life is more correctly measured in broad segments than tiny spans of time that may find me temporarily high or low.

Retirement is definitely a significant dividing point in most people's lives. Frankly, I find myself looking back as much as forward. I don't consider that sinful in spite of Paul's admonishment in Philippians 3:13-14 to press on.

In other places, such as 2 Corinthians 11:24-28, Paul does a lot of looking back. For me, at this particular point in life, I find it more advantageous to look back and see how straight a furrow I have plowed, how much ground I have covered. It's hard to go someplace unless you know from whence you came.

As I look back, it's not all bad. I feel more pleased than displeased. I know I have hit a few rocks, broken a few plow points, run out of gas a few times, misused the tractor upon occasion. I have even plowed on Sunday because I did not tithe my time correctly. Much of that past has been in God's hands—some of it, unfortunately, not. But such mistakes have been clarified with the Power above and I no longer worry about them.

The past does fall into neat segments. There were eighteen years of growing up, four years of college, four years of war, and forty years of teaching and marriage. Only the first and the last—growing up and marriage—continue. Ask me about any of the four and I will speak to you with some authority. Just don't ask me how retirement is going.

I am in transition. I tell people, "My wife has given me a year to unwind." That's not quite true. But she has mandated little from me just yet, except to carry the garbage to the compost heap. And I have been able to handle that. I often go out to my bees that are near the heap anyway, so I feel her commands are gentle thus far.

I see a sharp glint in her eyes, however, as she prowls around the residence, noting areas for repair, finishing, and refinishing. So far, I have simply moved the newspaper up a little higher to block her questioning glance. Or slunk into my study, closed the door, punched a few keys of the typewriter at random and sporadically for effect as I read a library book.

I think the retirement chapter will be a good one. I look forward to it like I do to a trip, with wonderment as to what God will bring about during the next fifteen, twenty, twenty-five years. To look back is, as I intimated, good. To stay there is bad. I have often quoted that roundheaded boy, Charlie Brown of the comic strip "Peanuts." When questioned about his favorite day of the week, he replied, "I've always been kind of fond of tomorrow."

Soap Operas, Grandchildren, Etc. (1989)

People are bugging me again.

Before retirement the common question was, "When are you going to retire?" Behind the question I heard, "You are a money-grubbing school teacher who has taught long past his prime. Yet you hang in there, keeping younger, more effective teachers from the classroom. Stop working!"

The last years I taught I did so knowing the local school board would have preferred hiring a young, green teacher for $15,000 over retaining a faded brown one costing twice that much. The school administration dangled financial carrots in front of aging teachers, tempting them to retire early, quit working. The "when" of retirement came up more frequently than a weather report.

I called it quits. Dinosaur Baker trudged off the battlefield to lick his wounds in retirement. The thundering lizard era ended as the know-it-all mammals came on the scene.

Now, behold, a new question has arisen. It seems the antithesis, nearly opposite, of the question asked me before retirement. I am constantly being interrogated with the question, even flogged with it: "What are you doing in retirement?"

How strange! Before the magic retirement date, I heard people say, "Stop working." Now I hear them say, "What are you working at?" It's tough to win.

I am thinking up a variety of smart-aleck, chilling, antisocial answers. Once they circulate, I hope people will leave me alone in what they probably feel are my retirement sins and stop worrying about me.

I could easily learn about the afternoon TV soap operas by studying for thirty minutes each week the synopsis-like summary laid out neatly in our local newspaper. Without viewing a single soap, I could easily and quickly get the gist of *All My Children*, *Days of Our Lives*, *As the World Turns*, and *General Hospital*. No need to watch them to follow those simplistic plots which, I understand, stretch a 15-minute life happening into six months of TV pap and pulp.

When questioned about my gainful employment during retirement, I could say with enthusiasm, with animation, "Man, I'm into the soaps. They're the greatest." While listeners gasped, I could mention the thin plot of *One Life to Live* or *Guiding Light*.

Then I would hit them with my pitch. "I have three VCRs and tape everything from Monday through Friday. That way I can watch them again in the morning. I'm running a video tape service where I rent out video copies to subscribers."

Then I would grab the lapels of my questioner

(or handbag, if female), and beg, "Could I sell you a subscription? You furnish the blank tapes and I do them for $20 per week. It keeps me off welfare, and it keeps you up with your favorite soaps. Please, pretty please?"

Or I could fill a large, three-ring notebook with pictures of our seven grandchildren, each child having a series of, perhaps, five pictures from birth until now. I would have records of their accomplishments—when they crawled, when they walked, their first words. I would make graphs of their changes in weight and height. For the ones in school, I could have copies of their report cards, honors won, hobbies, and instruments played.

I would keep that notebook with me always, ready for the question, "What are you doing in retirement?" Instantly I would pop open the notebook with the happy words, "So glad you asked. I've become a chronicler of my grandchildren. You will love these."

Then I would insist they sit down with me while I, with doting-grandfather enthusiasm, would go tediously through the book. I would have a tape recorder with me so I could play a tape of each child talking (or crying, in case of the babies) as I showed them the appropriate pictures.

After an hour or so, when my questioner had begun to edge away, citing innumerable appointments, I would say, "Oh, but I have a lot more to show you about the grandchildren. I have a thirty-minute home video of each. Should I come to your house, or would you like to come to mine?"

I think the word would spread, pretty quickly, among those worried about what I am doing during retirement. "Baker," they would say, "has gone off the deep end about his grandchildren."

Another ploy I am considering could profit the church. When that tainted question about my suspected loafing—as I drained Social Security dry—came up, I could say, "Oh, did you not know that I am the sole representative for BMSFRCMW in this area?" While they are still gasping, I would explain the acronym stood for Board of Missions Special Fund for Retired City Mission Workers.

I could make up some brochures myself, citing the need of one or two city mission workers, and flash it by my victim. I would produce a receipt book and generic checks, in case they tried to weasel out of giving because they did not have their checkbook with them. Any money collected, I would give to charity.

I am certain there are dozens of creative ways to silence those jealous, crafty probers of my retirement activities. After a couple of the above confrontations, the word would get around. I would be treated as a normal person, not some recluse who is sitting at home doing nothing.

The grandchildren notebook and the mission worker brochure should be ready in thirty days. The TV soap retort is ready now, since it demands no props, just words. Once I'm in production, I figure a lot of people are going to think twice before they ask Bob Baker what he's doing to keep busy in retirement.

V

Views of Work:
Before and
After Retirement

My wife says I am a workaholic, a charge I categorically deny. I simply feel uncomfortable trying to do nothing, which in itself is an impossibility. You can do something, but you cannot do nothing.

When I began teaching, I quickly discovered pupils in my classes with Cadillac capacities, who threatened to leave my Model T intellect in the dust. I began running just to stay even as they walked. Since then I have found it hard to break the habit.

I did not feel that retirement from teaching was a mandate to take up thumb twirling and TV babysitting. Retirement has allowed me to continue and enlarge my hobbies of reading, writing, beekeeping. I have found it possible now to do more volunteer work, to serve the church during the week as well as on Sunday.

I confess that, as I age, my coffee breaks stretch longer, I tire more quickly, I am less organized. After forty years of hard labor in the classroom, a forty-hour week dotted with frequent R and R (rest and recreation) seems like duck soup. I still work but the retirement schedule is relaxed and sane.

Redeeming the Time

Come with me two and a half miles south of our home on County Road 13, then one and a quarter miles east on County Road 30, sometimes called Bashor Chapel Road. On our left will be an old, red brick farmhouse. We go up the lane to reach the pasture. At the end of the lane we come to the cemetery, "my cemetery." The gate is doubly secured, so we untie the rope and slide back the bar.

We enter the half-acre, little country cemetery. Immediately to the right we find the two gray tombstones bearing the names Jacob Leer and Margaret Leer. There lie Grandmother Rensberger's parents, my great-grandparents. Immediately behind the two stones, in the next plot, you will find my great-great grandparents, David and Elizabeth Leer.

"Big deal," you say, "Who cares?'

Ah, it is the thought that occurs in the cemetery which is important, not the people who lie buried there.

Over twenty-five years ago, my wife, in her genealogical research, discovered the cemetery. It had reverted back into wilderness. Our family reclaimed it from jungle-like conditions and saw that it was fenced. Now I mow it. Thus it becomes, "my cemetery."

Anna Mae has long said that another should care for the place. But the township will only do so if a veteran is buried there. So far, we cannot prove that, so I clip around the ancient stones. I find it a form of therapy, mowing in the hot sun, sweat streaming, thoughts swimming. In many ways the cemetery becomes a couch, and God my psychiatrist.

As I mow, a two-and-a-half-hour session, I nearly always have the same thought in the early rounds with the power mower. *This time, these particular moments I spend mowing today, will never occur again. They are singular, unique, at a tiny spot on God's time line for me, never to be repeated.*

It is a sobering thought to consider, time running like sand through one's fingers, grains dropping, irretrievably gone, never to be handled again. Tomorrow's time is not the same as today's. While the thoughts linger, I mow with seriousness and contemplation. I mow, reviewing and evaluating my use of time.

They say time is a talent given to each of us. My sixth-grade teacher at Samuel Strong School each week placed some thought gem on the blackboard. One I remember was "Lost yesterday, somewhere between sunrise and sunset, two golden hours, each set with sixty diamond minutes. No reward is offered, for they are gone forever." A half century old and Ms. Teed's blackboard sentence from Horace Mann still speaks to me.

The number 168 is almost a sacred number with me. It is the number of hours in a week. I juggle those 168 hours. I squeeze, manipulate, even cheat at times. But I have no hope, like Joshua, of making the sun stand still (Josh. 10:12-14). Time is a commodity we sell too cheaply.

The present is spinning irreversibly into the past; it will never be repeated.

Each hour is golden. Each moment should sparkle like a diamond. Time is a treasure chest of riches poured out to us. The golden flood seems endless, engulfing.

The days slip by, the hours disappear, the minutes evaporate, the seconds dissolve. At the end of the day, we often hold in our minds only collapsed and empty bubbles that once held time treasures we wasted. Like the prodigal son, we spend our inheritance in "riotous living."

Time is the most precious asset I have. It far exceeds my savings account, my IRAs, my pitiful CDs, the scant tax-deferred annuity plan I began about the year I should have been completing it.

Someone else has said what I believe, though his identity remains unknown.

> If you had a bank that credited your account each morning with $86,400 that carried over no balance from day to day, allowed you to keep no cash in your account, and every evening canceled whatever part of the amount you had failed to use during the day, what would you do? Draw out every cent, of course! Well, you have such a bank, and its name is

"time." Every morning it credits you with 86,400 seconds. Every night it rules off, as lost, whatever of this you have failed to invest to good purpose. It carries over no balances. It allows no overdrafts. Each day it opens a new account with you. Each night it burns the records of the day. If you fail to use the day's deposits, the loss is yours. There is no going back. There is no drawing against the "tomorrow." You must live in the present on today's deposits. Invest it so as to get from it the utmost in health, happiness, and success!

So I continue to mow "my" cemetery and think about time. I want to be living, working, and thinking productively every day of my life. More of it is used up now than remains. But I expect no Hezekiah extension as in 2 Kings 20. The only time I have is this precious, fleeting moment of *now*. I grasp it greedily. To waste it is sin.

Following J. S.

When J. S. Hartzler, veteran church leader, appeared at a Mennonite assembly in 1945, his craggy features were marred by scrapes and scratches. Several of his ministerial brethren wondered why and went to ask him.

Brother J. S. explained that he had slipped and fallen over a wheelbarrow while tidying up his yard on Prairie Street in Elkhart. At that time he was eighty-eight years old.

One who heard that explanation was Wilbur Yoder. He decided to give his older brother some tactful advice in regard to being more careful at such a fragile age.

"Brother J. S.," said Wilbur, "I am not old enough to give you advice. But if I were, I would suggest you ought to know better than to be tackling such a job. You should leave such tasks to others." Wilbur said this respectfully, with genuine concern.

The patriarch was not impressed. "I have noticed something in this town when railroad personnel retire. First, we see their retirement pictures in the paper. Usually within a year, we read their obituaries. They retire from an active life into nothingness. I propose to do no such thing."

For me, J. S. Hartzler put his finger on something that we maturing ones need to look at carefully, regardless of which side of eighty-eight we are on.

Like a car, the body seems to function best if it is used periodically—revved up a bit to clear the carbon from the engine. When we move from the exhilaration and satisfaction that come due to the activity of a daily job and move into a vacuum, something is bound to collapse. The old adage "Nature abhors a vacuum" has been tossed out of the world of physics. But it does have a bearing on the physical life.

So, at my age, I keep pushing myself. Long ago I gave up maintaining my youthful facial appearance. But I am selfish about both my brain and physical prowess. There is no magic age at which they wither.

I can still hear my first Sunday school superintendent, C. W. Leininger, saying, "I would sooner burn out than rust out." I have accepted his philosophy. There are worse things than being an ancient workaholic.

Physically and mentally, I want to keep limber. At seventy, God has blessed me with good health, so I use it, refusing to wrap it in a napkin. If my brain cells are decreasing, I simply work the remaining ones harder.

When I was fifty-eight, I became concerned about the energy situation and was anxious to set a good example as a science teacher. So I began riding a bicycle to school, a distance of 4.6 miles. I am certain that some along my route, watching me ride through the rain or zero weather, labeled me a "kook." Let them.

I still mow the half-acre cemetery lot for which we have assumed responsibility because no one else did. And I mow our own lawn, another half acre plus.

I like to go to bed dog-tired. In the morning I try not to growl, even though my muscles do for the first ten minutes. (It seems no matter how often I use some of them, they like to complain. Maybe it's because they are Mennonite muscles.)

Contrary to what some people think and believe, not all schoolteachers take three-month vacations while teaching. I set work quotas for myself, goals that I hoped to reach. During the summer, I pounded out writing assignments in advance. Then when school started in the fall, I could give 110 percent to my teaching.

That's right, 110 percent. Like other minorities, I worked harder to prove I could do it. Older persons have to do so. At my school, with fifty faculty members, I was the second or third to arrive, occasionally first. Often among the last to leave.

As I mature, I try to do a little more than the next person, not less. Do I sound a bit boastful? Or worse, pertly self-assertive, conceited, even arrogant?

I prefer to call it justifiable egotism. Something each of us needs in some amount, regardless of our age. Each of us needs to think reasonably well of ourselves. I do not worry about getting too "biggity." God has let the air out of my ego balloon so often I can't count the patches.

So I think J. S. Hartzler was no dummy. Like him, I intend to push the wheelbarrow, not ride in it.

The mind is meant to be free, fertile, and fruitful—always. The body is fantastic, flexible, and faithful, if not abused or diseased. Both function best when pushed a bit. And I think I have a mite of biblical support: "Whatsoever thy hand findeth to do, do it with thy might" (Eccles. 9:10, KJV).

I see no age exclusion in that verse. So I'll take my chances on whether pushing myself adds to or takes from my life.

Frankly, I prefer wearing out at seventy to wasting away at eighty. I prefer mobility and the coronary at seventy to the stroke at eighty and that twilight zone when I am neither here nor there.

My leaving time and mode of departure I leave to God. But I do not think it hurts to give him my preference now, so he can make a note of it. He has a lot on his mind and shouldn't resent my reminder.

After Retirement, I Switched

When I retired from teaching, I said "no" to having my name on any substitute teacher list. I wanted to cut the strings sharply, permanently. Substitutes live a rough life and are an endangered species. I planned to forget school, pupils, teachers, principals, even the custodian.

Then Sherm Kauffman called to sweet-talk me into going back to school, but wearing a different hat. Bethany Christian High School had a vacancy on its board. Would I fill it?

Rather than give the quick, emphatic "no," which was my immediate response, I said, "Let me think about it." One should not be ungracious, but the appeal to me was microscopic. My animal nature would allow me to play possum for a week or so, ferret out an excuse, then weasel out of the offer.

Admittedly, I did think about the job. I wondered how many people they called and received negative responses from before they got to me. I was too proud to ask. I could hear Sherm saying, "Well, Bob, to be perfectly honest, you were number thirty-two—we're desperate, mighty desperate."

Or could it have been an honest call, but actually they wanted someone to write up the minutes of their endless board meetings. I would be a member of the board. Silent, yes, but expected to legitimize board ramblings by reducing them to profound statements for release to the press, the church, and the historical archives.

Besides, as a classroom teacher, I have always been suspicious of school boards. They are like generals in the Pentagon, preparing battle plans for those in the trenches. They don't know what it's like to be on the front lines, to hear the shot and shell whistling overhead. Yet they are great at firing out verbal orders, sending privates into the jaws of death. Why would I want to change sides, join the enemy, so to speak? I am more intelligent than I look.

I knew a few people on the school board. They all seemed young, terribly young. At sixty-seven, I wondered if I was to be the token senior, stirred into the pot of intellectual stew like some wrinkled cabbage leaves to satisfy the gray-power advocates. I could see other board members holding doors open for me, giving me the soft seat. They would continually inquire if I could hear properly and hasten to get me a glass of water every time I cleared my throat.

But even if all of the above were correct, might there not be some perks? Maybe it would be interesting to sit on the other side of the fence after forty years on one side. I saw the school board as made up of professional people, financiers, doctors, ministers. They would be people who had never tried to take on thirty or forty wild teenagers, people who would wonder about the significance of teachers calling Wednesday "over the hump day." At last I would know what it meant to "teach school," as I learned how to run a school from the board's perspective.

A couple of other things drew me. Three of our five children had gone to the school. We had a bundle of money invested there in the form of tuition. Maybe I should invest three years of my own life in the place.

Early in our marriage Anna Mae and I were living on a beginning teacher's salary. She was working full-time as a mother and housewife. Back then I had to go to the bank to get a loan on the car before I could bail my wife out of the hospital, where she was going with some regularity to have babies.

At that point, a church leader sounded me out as a potential teacher for Bethany. We were living on a shoestring, a torn and knotted shoestring, and I knew teachers at Bethany would have even less. We turned away from the possibility. Maybe I should now make up for the years I never gave to Bethany.

I called up Bill Hooley, head honcho at Bethany. He kindly set up an appointment to discuss Sherm Kauffman's offer. He told me what he expected from a school board member, affirmed me in my gifts, thought I could make a contribution to Bethany. This gentle, discerning, dedicated brother was very convincing.

I accepted.

It has been an interesting experiment. The ball game is a different one, yet in some ways the same. I have seen some of the worries that come with running a school. You worry about finances, teacher morale and salaries, building plans, faulty heating systems. I came to the board teacher-oriented, biased. I haven't changed.

I've made mistakes on the board. I've had my surprises. I've bumped into some differences with board members, even disagreed with Bill Hooley, something I formerly thought was impossible. I've been the lone dissenting vote, the obstinate one. But others have respected my negativeness or done an excellent job hiding their disgust.

One learns about retirement by retiring. It is best not to make dogmatic statements about the future. James warns against it, saying it is stupid to say what you are going to do tomorrow. Temper such statements with "If the Lord will" (4:13-15, KJV).

I said I would forget school. Nonsense. I could not eliminate the past by making rash statements. I do not tell God what I will or will not do.

I must submit. If I do not, God shrugs his shoulders, smiles sadly, murmurs questioningly, "How can you be my disciple if you act as if you are Lord?"

Retirement is not for selfish pleasure, a time for resting, rusting. It is a time to dare, adventure, experiment. Fine. Suits me, even if it means serving on a school board.

Bag Man for the Hungry

I have probably drained more beer cans to the last drop this past year than any reader. In the process, I have been the recipient of more pitying looks than any person likely to read this book.

And I am certain that some who read this will shake their head as they consider the degradation to which I have fallen. What shame for those who know me. And how must my wife feel? On the other hand, my apparent downfall lies at her feet.

Yet I must bear some of the blame. No one forced me into becoming a bag man. It has been profitable to me, a learning process, somewhat humbling. I have seen pictures in the paper or magazines, viewed documentaries on TV about the homeless and scattered of our large cities. I am pained by views of elderly women, often dirty, unkempt, pushing grocery carts or carrying shopping bags that contain their worldly belongings.

Such a person is sometimes called a bag woman. This is sad, a reflection on a society that contains unfairness, inequalities. They deserve more than our pitying looks.

In a small way, I have identified with them. For six months I have roamed, not the streets of New York City, but the county highways of Elkhart County, Indiana. And I have carried a black plastic bag while trudging the berms, looking in the grass, the ditches, picking up aluminum cans.

As I said, it's partly, perhaps mainly, my wife's fault that I became a bag man. While I was pedaling my bicycle to school, she exercised by walking at the nearby mall, a mile from our home. When I retired, I thought the absence of the ten-mile round trip to school would make little difference in my life. But it did. My pants began to shrink. My belt grew shorter. I began to waddle. My more or less rotund figure became definitely more rotund.

My wife suggested I walk with her at the mall. I did. I covered three or four miles a day, memorized window displays, and was tempted to buy everything from pianos to goldfish.

It helped. But I, who formerly exercised with the purpose of getting myself to and from school, was left thinking, *I wish I could sense more purpose in this walking.*

When the weather improved, sometimes I walked to the mall as a part of the morning's exercise. On the way, I noticed aluminum cans. I recalled telling my students in earth science that the aluminum industry saved 95 percent of the energy required to make the metal originally when using recycled aluminum.

So I began carrying a small plastic bag with me when I walked to the miniature city. When I found a can, I shook the last few alcoholic drops or sweet sugar from it and carried it home.

One thing often leads to another. When the weather was nice—I like fresh air better than stale —why not skip the mall, walk around the square? Surely I would find more aluminum cans. I did.

And why not go beyond the square? I did not have to walk the same route each day. Why not explore new county roads? I did. Business picked up; I was mining new areas. Anna Mae looked apprehensively at the plastic sacks of aluminum cans beginning to accumulate behind the garage.

As I walked, I thought, got new ideas. Although we were on retirement income, there was enough. I did not really need the income from selling aluminum cans. So I decided one morning—why not sell the cans, give the money to Mennonite Central Committee for world relief? Sounded good.

It must have sounded good to the Lord also. He said to me, "I like it! Only one suggestion: You could also match from your own pocket the sum you get from the cans. Then MCC would have twice the amount."

"Whoa, Lord. You mean match my can money with tithe money? We don't have that much tithe money since I retired from that rich teaching job."

"Of course not. You know what I mean. Match it out of that 90 percent of the income you have been hogging from Social Security and your teacher's pension."

I wanted to question. But that morning it was cloudy, rain was threatening, and I thought I heard a bit of thunder. I quickly agreed.

After six months of walking/collecting, I sold my aluminum mountain. I had eighty-two pounds of cans. The cans run about twenty-five to the pound, so that means I had picked up about 2,050 cans, minus a few contributed by neighbors.

That's a lot of cheap stoop labor. I now know how a migrant laborer feels, or at least about one percent of how he or she feels. Aluminum had just gone up to fifty cents a pound, so I received $41. I matched that and sent a check to Mennonite Central Committee for $82. I don't know what they thought about that odd sum, but they accepted it.

Frankly, I like what I did, what I will continue to do until the Lord changes the morning walk. What I do helps clean the environment. It saves electrical energy. It benefits the poor of the world. And it makes my walking pay off. I do my walking in the morning. I have four routes I try to follow, most of them about five miles in length.

I walk a mile in twenty minutes, so I am out about an hour and a half. My wife frowns at the time spent. But I tell her it is better than sitting around trying to run her household business. She is frowning less often.

I have mixed feelings about the impression I am making on those who view my antics. Do they see me as poverty-stricken, the poor, old, retired school teacher who picks up cans to help make ends meet? A few drivers wave. Some friends even acknowledge me. Others look straight ahead.

Am I an unpleasant reminder of a part of America they wish would go away? Of course, I keep no record, no inventory of every driver's face. Many I do not even see. As you know, Mountain Dew and Seven-Up cans are green, and one needs to keep a sharp eye out for them in the grass.

Some mornings the pickings are scant. I return with only five or six cans. But other times I may hit a beer or soft-drink mother lode. Then I strike it rich and bring back twenty or thirty.

There are other rewards. I have found valuables by the roadside, including a fine T square, a good sweatshirt, tools for my toolbox. Once a dollar bill the wind had pinned against the fence sat waiting for me to pluck it off.

My biggest strike was in a dumpster. Yes, I've crawled into a few when the can pickings were good. Dumpsters really aren't so bad. In the one that gave me the biggest thrill, the one behind a nearby school, I found a neat, clean, brown envelope. Curious, I opened it. There were over thirty dollars in there, plus over a hundred dollars in uncashed checks.

I turned it in at the school. The administrators were triply amazed: first, that it was discarded; second, that I found it; and third, that I returned it.

As I walk I dream of organizing a host of retired Christians. We walk the highways, bag men, bag women for the Lord.

I dream of churches collecting aluminum cans from members, charging admission in cans on Sunday morning. Let's see, we could charge five cans for a regular sermon—seven if there is special music. Even ten if the preacher promised a short sermon. Or should it be ten cans for a long sermon? Well, we could work that out.

VI

Walking with the
Cancer Patient

I like to laugh, help people smile, chuckle. I believe God has a good sense of humor. He must to deal with us, such odd, funny parts of his creation.

But there is no laughter in this section of our journey. Skip these chapters if you would avoid tears.

As we grow older we attend more funerals. Dying is normal. It is to be anticipated. But when death comes to our friends, especially to one of the family, we are never quite prepared.

So it was for me when my sister Helen died after a long bout with cancer which intensified just at the time of my retirement. It was as if God waited for me to be free so I could minister to Helen. For that I am deeply grateful.

The whole process was a learning experience punctuated with hope, prayers, fear, pain, anger, trust. Each time I pass her old home, where others now live, or touch the church bench where we sat together, memories flood back. Living and dying, dying and living are inseparably linked.

Being a resource to Helen changed me. I complain less. I try to celebrate life without ignoring death. I remind myself earth is not my home; I am just passing through.

Our Bout with Magnetic Resonance Imaging

My sister Helen and I were amateurs; we had no experience in acting. We were willing to let God write the script, each playing the role assigned. We knew God stood behind the side stage curtain, prompting, directing, supporting us in our roles.

Act One, Scene One, took place at the Magnetic Resonance Imaging Center in South Bend, Indiana. It was a biggie. For a short time, I thought Helen might refuse to go on stage.

Enter a brochure. It was light gray with the silhouette of a person on the front in darker gray. The title read "A Patient's Guide to Understanding Magnetic Resonance Imaging."

On the back, boxed in so we couldn't miss it, were the specifics of our appointment: "Your MRI scan is scheduled for Tuesday, August 4, 1987. Please arrive at the Center by 11:15. Bring this brochure and any forms that your doctor has given you." Below the appointment box was a map showing the location of the Center.

I read the brochure several times and thought I knew something about what was to happen.

Magnetic resonance imaging distinguishes between healthy and diseased tissue without the aid of contrasting dyes or use of X-rays. It can reduce the need for extensive testing and can actually "see" through bone, providing detailed images of soft tissue.

A photo of the machine made it look massive, complicated, futuristic. The examination was to be painless. Restrictions? No jewelry, watches, hairpins, clips, dentures, glasses, hearing aids, coins, credit cards, keys. Any implanted metal objects were to be reported to the attendant. A locker was provided for the removable metallic objects.

I was leery of the machine. The picture and instructions showed that the patient to be scanned would be placed on a narrow table. The table would be put into the center of a larger cylinder-shaped magnet.

This would give Helen, my sister, trouble. The brochure warned of it: "A small number of patients who suffer from claustrophobia may tend to feel 'closed in' or be bothered by the knocking noise they hear during the scan." My sister, who was sentenced by the cancer specialist to have a scan done, suffered from claustrophobia. Yet the scan needed to be done prior to the radiation that was to follow.

So, the day before the examination, on August 3, I visited my sister, brochure in hand. Upon learning of the growing malignancy in her abdomen, Helen made me her confidant. She trusted me, sought my advice. After all, college graduates, especially those who have taught for forty years, are very wise.

She had a right to know, before we went for the exam, what would happen. She was seventy-three years old, perfectly alert, and could not be treated like a child. She needed to know that she would be inserted into the machine, walled in except at the two ends. She would be confined in the cylinder for forty-sixty minutes. I expected problems when I detailed what she should expect. I was right.

When I explained, Helen rose from her chair, visibly shaken. She walked out of the room, saying as she passed me, "Well, you can just call them up and cancel the appointment. I can't do it." I wheedled her into at least keeping the appointment.

On the fourth of August we arrived at the Center on time. I had called the staff earlier to let them know of Helen's reluctance. They were understanding. They promised a sedative and that I would be allowed in the scanning room with her.

After preparation, we stood before the machine. For me, it was fascinating—for Helen, frightening. After two intravenous injections, she was willing.

The machine was remote-controlled from an observation and recording room. We were alone in the scanning room—Helen in the machine, myself beside it. I stood at her feet, and we could see one another. We could talk with each other and were in communication electronically with the doctor and machine operators.

As the scanning began, I felt my plastic-frame glasses responding to the magnetic pull, even though I was outside the machine. The tiny hinges were of metal. I thrust the glasses deep into the case and my pocket, fearing they would leap from me to my sister. I suppose the fear was needless, but it was one more thing to impress me with the power before me.

The testing was completed. The technicians said, "We got some good pictures." I was proud of my sister. She had successfully passed her first test on a long and wavering journey toward arresting the wild growth of cells within. I planned, God willing, to walk with her on the journey.

The specialist, the one ordering the magnetic resonance imaging, was cautiously optimistic. Daily radiation for four to six weeks followed. In the midst of our pain and sorrow, our fears at the length of the unknown valley before us, I heard Helen's plaintive cry: "I thought when you were older, you could relax, enjoy yourself. Now this."

I had no profound answers, nothing except, "Helen, we have to trust God. We must go one step at a time, take each day as it comes."

In all our questioning, there was a solacing thought. My sister and I were both Christians and we knew God who would never leave us.

A New Word—Oncology

You have the flu, with all its accompanying miseries. Your nose runs, your bones ache, your head throbs. Your food can't make up its mind which way it should go—it slows, then accelerates without rhyme or reason. You feel miserable.

You have had a hernia operation, can't sit down, can't stand up. You spent over an hour on the operating table, four days on the La-Z-Boy chair. You take pain pills to sleep. The gigantic Band-Aid the surgeon slapped across your belly covers a four-inch incision, red and angry, painful. You'd like to be left alone so you can grimace the pain away and enjoy periods of self-pity.

What you need, instead, is a swift kick on your posterior. You have as much reason to be depressed as a bee in a clover field.

I am sick and tired of hearing people, including myself, complain of little aches, pains, and frustrations. I'm sick of the pity parties we hold because we are too thin in the face, too fat in the belly, too flat on our feet. Enough of acting as if a twenty-four-hour virus is the bubonic plague, weeping over minutiae, blowing up trifles like so much bubble gum, making mountains out of molehill ailments and disappointments.

Pardon my anger, even my rage. I have not always been this way. I do not know how long I will stay this way, quivering in righteous indignation because of childish bellyaching by adults. Although I include myself as one who has majored in microscopic minors, I hope I am changing. I hope I am becoming a believer in that old line of confession, "I complained because I had no shoes until I saw a man who had no feet."

My attempt to change started at Memorial Hospital, South Bend, Indiana, Oncology Department.

"Oncology?" I did not even know what the word meant before last summer. It was a camouflage word, a word with hidden meaning. They posted it on the sign just beyond the main entrance to the hospital, giving only a hint of both the promises and sorrows that lay within the beautiful glass-brick building.

The sign reads "Radiation-Oncology Visitor Parking." The word *radiation* hints at the meaning of oncology. The dictionary more fully describes it: "The part of medical science that treats of tumors." It comes from a Greek word meaning "bulk, mass." A loose translation: "Cancer." Cancer—malignant growth, fearful cells that refuse to be governed by orderly growth, cells that crowd, dominate, demand, assert, drain.

We visit the oncology section of the hospital because of cancer. It is my sister, widowed, alone. . . .

Cancer is not a four-letter word, one to speak only in whispers, something to be ignored. Cancer is not a deliberate curse of God, a punishment for sin. But it must be faced.

Four weeks of radiation is not pleasant for the one radiated. I read the booklets, publications of the National Institutes of Health, entitled *Radiation Therapy and You* and *Taking Time*. They were both helpful. Because of her poor vision I read and explained them to my sister. They forewarned of nausea, loss of appetite, fatigue, diarrhea. They were good prophets.

Members of the family, friends, took Helen to South Bend for the daily treatments. As a family, we wanted and were happy to assume major responsibility. So I was often in the waiting room of the oncology department while the radiation was being given.

And once a week, as the nearest relative, I listened with Helen to good Dr. Schneider as he checked and counseled with the patient. The doctor spoke aloud. The waiting room spoke silently. I remember as if it were yesterday.

The waiting room is usually full. We are the car drivers, often relatives, spouses, children, siblings. We deliver, we wait. Some patients walk in, the picture of health. Some are wheeled in; some come with canes or crutches. Some women with bandannas around their heads speak of previous chemotherapy, of radiation to the head area.

We who wait for those we brought in are wondering, questioning, hopeful people, trying to stay up in the cancer quicksand around us.

We are close to those we bring, but we cannot see inside their minds. We cannot sense fully their own hopes and fears. We may be burdened for those we brought, but our load is small compared to the one they carry. We can compare the weight the one with cancer carries with the frivolous complaints we hear from those who moan about the insignificant. And it angers us, we of the waiting room.

The waiting room is quiet. We can read, watch TV, talk quietly, stare into space, scan the room. It is not a happy room. Smiles are limited. The TV has to be pretty funny to provoke grins. It is a room without laughter.

We look discreetly at our companions, fellow car drivers, transporters. Some impress us more than others. My eyes lock with those of a young lady on a particular day. Her eyes glisten. They are filled with tears she wills not to flow. Mine fill also. Finally we both look away. Now, months later, I wonder if I should not have gone over, held her hand, let her unload, spill the tears.

Once while waiting, I met an old teacher friend, Nellie. Years ago, I had visited her in the Elkhart General Hospital when she had her first cancer operation. There had been a recurrence; she was back for radiation. Our meeting here was totally unexpected. She was so happy to see me—why, I don't know. She was probably in her late seventies, early eighties, thin as a wisp.

She clung to me, weeping. And I wept too, no repression this time. The waiting room occupants understood. We were sojourners together in a land that at times offered hope. Pain and fear accompanied us. Hope flitted about us, evaded tight grasp. It tantalized, now dancing closely, now skittering away. It was hope not realized, wavering, almost as if teasing, yet never dying, a warming sun on a distant horizon—but we were cold.

That summer affected me, hardened me against the whiner, the complainer. I want to scream at the one who moans loudly over midget matters, who complains bitterly because the toast is overdone, the paper is late, the TV picture is snowy, the favorite ball team loses.

It has been a time of correcting myself, of learning to count blessings instead of complaints. I have much to learn.

So that year I learned a new word: oncology. For those who know of it, have suffered, are walking the gray miles, I have a new empathy. I weep with you.

"Dear Helen"

I promised that I would walk with you on your cancer journey. It has been a long walk, stretching over many years. For the last three, the walk has become more serious, more strenuous, more painful. And we walked more slowly, I your brother, you my sister.

There was the walk through the cancer operation, through radiation, through chemotherapy. Did I walk close enough to you, Helen? Was I there when you needed me? Don't answer; I know—sometimes, but not always. Sometimes I was selfish.

You were six years older than I. You were the oldest of seven children, the fourth to go, leaving three behind. You were the giver, the sharer, the contributor.

When Father died, you quit school and went to work to help Mother. You worked seven days a week, ten hours a day, for seven dollars. Each week you gave mother five dollars, kept two for yourself. Those were the depression years and every dollar helped. I was twelve then and thought little of the sacrifice you made. Now, too late, I am reminded of it. I never said "Thanks" for what you did, assuming an adult role so young.

I think a lot now of the past three years. I think of the trips to South Bend for radiation. It was a long summer, full of trials and tribulations for you. You had to quit your job. That was painful, more painful than the problems brought on by the radiation.

We thought we had the cancer whipped. The young doctor spoke so hopefully. Just come back for a checkup every six weeks or so. Things are looking good.

False hope. On one of the checkups, he frowns. We need to see another specialist about this changing tissue of your abdomen. We joke about all the doctors you see. We do not laugh when he calls to give the results of tests from tissue extracted. Instead, we cry. Now we must see another doctor. He turns out to be nicest. But he will be the last.

He is Dr. William Pletcher, oncologist at the medical clinic. He is an active Christian layman, but frank, very frank. I have had his children in school and we are friends.

He studies the reports that accompany us from other doctors. He checks the medical descriptions, X-rays, magnetic resonance image pictures. Your folder is getting pretty thick. And he examines you in the office.

Then we sit down beside his desk. He is serious, very serious. The outlook is not good. What the radiation specialist had thought quenched was now flaring anew in ugly, spreading conflagration.

We ask for a prognosis. We are shocked when he says, "Four or five months, Helen. Perhaps."

We sit there stunned. Almost angrily I reply, "But doctors have been wrong before!" He humbly agrees. Then he does something few doctors do. He takes your hand and prays aloud for you.

Further appointments are made. He suggests, "There is a new drug out for this particular cancer." Even though the cancer has spread, he suggests we try the new drug. We clutch the straw.

So we go through August, September, October, November, December, into January. It is chemotherapy. There are injections, intravenous infusions, blood tests. Dr. Pletcher says he will settle for any of three possible options—complete elimination of the malignancy, reduction, or holding it at bay.

Every two weeks we are back at the clinic, checking blood cell counts. Platinum is dripped into your veins. You get CAT scans. Both of us hope, pray. The war is waged, battle by battle. You win some, lose some. Some weeks it is a draw.

Then in January comes the weakening. No appetite. Anna Mae accompanies me to the last appointment. We need moral support; it's wheelchair time.

Dr. Pletcher and nurse Diana Leatherman, both Christians, are loving. But medical science has reached the end of its string. You can stand no more. Gently the doctor says, "We want you to be comfortable. I would like to have hospice nurses call at the home." Agreed. What can you do but agree?

I remember so well that day, because it was an

extra heavy day for you. After leaving the clinic, Anna Mae and I took you to the funeral home in Goshen. There you viewed the body of Shane Sweisberger, your dearest friend. Then home to 1901 Yuma Street.

You wanted to die at home. I am glad it was possible. We stayed with you those last few days around the clock. And I still looked for the miracle. Three times before, in the last seven years, the doctors thought you would not make it. We proved them wrong. Not this time.

There was more than cancer. There was the heart problem and the emphysema. Anna Mae and I were both there the morning you slipped away so quietly we did not mark the exact moment, did not hear the flutter of the angels' wings.

I have regrets. You mentioned several weeks before your death the long, dark nights. I should have started staying with you at night earlier than I did. I thought it enough to drop in three or four times a day, leave at nine, leave you with the nights you disliked. I am sorry.

At times we were impatient with one another, spoke sharply. Remember the time we confessed that to one another, you standing over the hot air register, me beside you? We cried together, and it was healing.

I bugged and prodded you about eating, about using your oxygen. I wanted to feed you when you could still feed yourself. In my eagerness, I took dignity from you. Again, sorry!

But there were some good things. You started

coming to our church, Belmont Mennonite. You brought your membership there, experienced renewal in your Christian life. You found acceptance among the Mennonites. Few knew that you attended that church in your youth, left it for over fifty years, came back full circle.

You died in your chair, at home, without a struggle. And we were there. That cancels at least some of my regrets.

So our journey together is ended. I kept my promise to walk with you through your cancer journey. I walked as close as I could, most of the time. I miss so much the time we shared together, the loving things you did for us and others. Your leaving left a vacuum.

One hospice nurse called to see if I wanted to come in and talk about it. I said, "No. Maybe later."

I can't mail you this letter. Heaven has no zip code. Perhaps Jesus will share parts of this letter with you, the parts you need to hear.

Perhaps I wrote it as much for myself as for you.

Take care. I'll see you.

Your brother, Bob.

VII

Nursing Homes:
Plus and Minus

Sorry, another sad section. You have my permission to skip it. But that will not ease the pain you may face later—either for a loved one or yourself.

In "Tough Decisions" I share the struggle Anna Mae and I faced with Uncle Louis. The year was 1981 and we were in our sixties. Ten years earlier Grandpa Moyer had come to live with us. That was a good decision. We decided against Uncle Louis. Here we cannot be so certain we were right.

I feel better about Glenn and Roman. They were friends of mine who spent years in the nursing homes. I visited them, and the visits were rich experiences. The time I spent with them was siphoned from a busy schedule, but I regret not a second. The memories, years later, are irreplaceable.

An editor said, "Are you anti-nursing home?" Not at all. I am anti-people who feel that once a person is so placed, all obligation to them ends.

Retirement has let me be available to those not so mobile. Visiting them, taking flowers or some food delicacy, praying with them, or sending a cheerful card blesses me.

My retirement is a time to share.

Tough Decisions

"Outspoken" best describes my friend. And I refer not to his bicycling abilities. He has been labeled with much stronger words, some best not seen in print. I met him a dozen years ago, and we remain friends today. As in magnets, perhaps opposites attract!

One day we talked about care of the aged. He, in his usual blunt, stinging way, said, "I think the Mennonite Church made a mistake in building all the nursing centers and retirement communities. Old people need to be cared for in the homes of their children, of relatives and friends, not in institutions."

So much for all the planning, wisdom, and millions of investment dollars. But he had his reasons.

I have thought much about his views in recent years. Convalescent homes and nursing centers have been places I visit only sporadically. But now my wife and I have become more frequent visitors as we try to do what's best for an aging relative. Frankly, we found our first visits difficult, at times depressing.

Since visiting more frequently and staying longer, we see more and understand more.

We see lots of love and care by nurses, aides, social workers, and other personnel laboring with deep dedication at such nursing homes. We cannot fault a single one of them. In an overwhelming situation, they are not overwhelmed. Their patience with patients is obvious, magnificent.

But we also hear the silence, see the emptiness, sense the vacuum.

Questions ricochet off the walls and stab at County Road 13 visitors. Is this where the elderly belong? Is this my future home?

I go back ten years to when my wife's father came to our home to live. Grandpa Moyer was eighty-eight at that time. We cleared the spare room. There he spent the last nine months of his earthly life. When it became impossible for amateurs to nurse him, an ambulance came and took him to a local nursing home.

He died that night amidst tubes and strangers. If we would have known death was that close, we would have kept him here. Coma or no coma, his daughter and I would have shared with him the break between earth and heaven.

Our aged relative today is bewildered in his new residence. The ninety-four-year-old mind was once so alert and accurate. It preached the Word and guided a parish. Now it cannot comprehend the situation in which it finds itself.

We saw his failing in the last months yet were shocked how rapid it was. We grieved at the hurt he expressed when those failings said, "You cannot live by yourself." We also are hurt and bewildered. Our guilt pangs come to bite sharply for a moment, to grind grimly for an hour.

And I jump ahead twenty years. I wonder if there is a Boaz in my future, one who "shall be unto thee a restorer of thy life, and a nourisher of thine old age" (Ruth 4:15, KJV). Or will I be signed over to an institution?

But that's future. What about today? Should we take ninety-four-year-old Uncle Louis into our home?

Always with the question comes the recall, the memories, the recognition that we are now ten years older. When Grandpa came to live at our house, our movements centered about him. Even the children still at home had to take second place at times.

We surrendered, submitted, subjected ourselves to the aged one. And knew that for that time it was right, good. Today the task would be far greater. Our lives are more complicated, ourselves more aged. We know the rubber band can be stretched only so far without snapping.

So we struggle. Have we done enough? Could we push ourselves farther? Are we selfish with the slim remaining years that we jealously want to husband for ourselves?

Today we go to visit our relative at the nursing home. We speak to him, reason with him, walk with him, wheel him about the long corridors. There we view the empty faces that are waiting, waiting, waiting. Hands clasped, heads bent, eyes looking into a distant, retreating world of the past. There is no present, so how can there be a future?

Has the church done right? At sixty, at seventy, I am still a part of that church, and in the past I helped to shape the present. But where is the present for our friend?

Recently I saw slides of Amish homes, sometimes with two additions branching out from the original. They were architecturally strange, grotesque, yet loving and tender grandpa houses. My Amish brothers and sisters, with their simple living, have answered the questions, solved the problem in their way. For them it is so correct.

But what about the Mennonites who care not for the simple life, who rejoice at being delivered from it? Has the answer for us been the sterile rooms off the long corridors, the white incubators for aged children? Color my thoughts gray.

This is not simply to say that we erred. We have done what we must because of where we are. The error may have occurred earlier. Perhaps once again we have jumped too quickly on the world's bandwagon in regard to care of the aged.

That's why I find myself praying, "Lord, if you are taking orders, make mine a coronary, preferably the kind that gives one twenty-four hours of conscious grace after the initial blockage. There are always some last-minute arrangements to be made."

But I quickly add, "I'm not putting a 'please rush' on the request. I enjoy living. But please, Lord, no trip for me to the nursing home. My wife can ill afford the $3,000 or more monthly bill. Nor am I worth it."

I much prefer an early arrival in heaven over a long stopover at a nursing home. And that's no reflection on all those fine brothers and sisters who have graciously dedicated their lives to caring for the aged and dying. It's simply a matter of personal preference.

Finding Time for Glenn

A short distance from Kokomo, Indiana, I turned the windshield wiper up to high. It was a bad night for driving. Already I was running an hour late. Really, I was six hours behind where I wanted to be on November 20, 1982. Was it all because of that telephone call the night before? I think so.

The telephone call had started it. And six precious hours were chewed out of my Saturday afternoon. I had had things scheduled to do. And I was sure my wife had tasks unspoken that would have doubled the load.

But there was Glenn, retired schoolteacher, twelve years my senior, who had taught many years next to me at Pierre Moran Junior High School. Now he was ill, perhaps terminally, confined to a convalescent home in Kokomo. I had been down to visit him in August and always wanted to do it again. But time is like premium gas—expensive.

The Friday before I had called his wife. "How's Glenn?"

"Oh, Mr. Baker, not so good. He seems to be in regression."

"But he seemed to be alert, in such good spirits, when I was there in August."

"Mr. Baker, you don't know how much we as a family appreciated that visit. It perked him up."

Glenn's wife dumped a heavy load on me. Finally I got from her the address of his new convalescent home. I would send a card.

That Saturday morning I was writing at school, then off to a two-hour seminar at 10:00. I knew what the Lord was kicking around inside my head. I tried to silence him. God kept banging away at me, "Work Glenn in today."

I told God I could not. The schedule was too tight. The only loose spot I had promised myself was the relaxation of watching one quarter of the Notre Dame-Air Force football game. At the most, that would be thirty minutes. Surely I deserved that.

The Lord agreed but added, "I still think you ought to see Glenn today." It's a four-hour round trip to Kokomo from Elkhart, plus an hour to visit Glenn. Impossible. I had no spare five hours. Glenn must wait. Yet the thought persisted, so I would lay out the fleece.

Over bean soup at noon, I said without enthusiasm to Anna Mae, "I thought of going down to Kokomo today or tomorrow to visit Glenn."

Her reply was quick, concerned: "If you think you should, you ought to go." I always knew she was in partnership with God.

When I arrived at the convalescent home, Glenn was sleeping. Nurses awakened him. I wondered if he would even know me. But Glenn snapped his eyes open and said, "Why, it's Bob Baker. Of course, I know you." I felt better.

The nurses insisted on getting Glenn into his wheelchair. We could go down to the lounge and chat. I noted the restraints on Glenn. His wife had mentioned that he had the habit of trying to walk when he should not.

We sat and talked for well over an hour. Glenn is a Christian and was a conscientious science teacher. He had things to discuss and recall with me. He was alert and remembered things I had forgotten.

Over the loudspeaker came the announcement for supper. When I got up to leave, Glenn grasped my hand and said with deep earnestness, "You must stay and eat with me. You never have."

I protested. Anna Mae and I had planned a late supper together. Glenn insisted. I yielded.

Our trays came. His was well filled, mine a simple hot dog and coffee. Glenn said, "Bob, I want you to ask the blessing." Why not? I prayed aloud. Let the other lounge eaters wonder; who cared? Glenn and I needed it.

We ate and talked. Glenn had custard pie. He wanted to share it. Again, I protested. Again, he pleaded. So I cut it in two and took half. Glenn's face was joyous as he said, "I'm so glad you did that."

Finally, I took Glenn to his room. Now I really had to leave. He grasped my hand with an iron grip. We looked into one another's face, crying. Glenn expressed his gratitude. I kissed his cheek, he kissed mine. Finally, I pried his hand off.

At the door I waved, then walked down the hall. For some reason, I went back. Glenn was still waving, eyes clenched shut, face twisted like a child who was lost. In one sense he was lost, separated, alone.

It was too much. I waved again in case he could see me. Then I fled, hurrying down the sterile hall, past the lounge where sat the helpless, silent, gray ones, past the busy rushing ones in white, and out. But outside I was still not safe. The pain remained.

I stopped at a shopping center, called Anna Mae, then scurried northward. From Kokomo to U.S. Highway 6 it is a straight shot, four lanes. I could drive and talk with God. God asked if I was happy about the schedule that day. I confessed that it was right, real right. God was happy, so was I, though my happiness was tinged with sadness.

I flicked on the radio to catch the news. At the close, they gave college football scores. Notre Dame, who was to be a sure winner over Air Force, got clobbered thirty-seventeen. I thought of the bumper stickers I saw in South Bend "God Made Notre Dame #1."

"Not today," I said.

Then came a happy, satisfied thought: "Today God made Glenn #1 in my life."

I felt good.

Meeting Jesus in Room 84

My last visit with Roman Gingerich was in December. He died less than a month later, in January.

As usual, in December we talked. Well, to be honest, only I talked, Roman listened. And as in previous visits, he gazed studiously at me with that quizzical look of his, head cocked to one side.

I could almost hear him say, "Now, I know you, but I can't quite place you. Give me a bit more time and maybe I can label you." I received more from Roman than I ever gave. Roman was a giver.

It was about four or five years ago that I called Roman for some advice about the use of Bee-go. This is a liquid that turns to a gas and can be used to drive bees down from a super of honey you want to remove from the hive.

I only wanted advice, but Roman said, "Look, I'll come over and help you, show you how to do it." Roman was a second-miler.

I still recall the warm August day he drove up the driveway. We put on our bee veils and talked while he got things out of the trunk of his car. As he rummaged around, he laughed and told me about purchasing that particular used car. On the used car lot, the first thing he checked was the trunk. It surprised the salesman. Most potential car buyers want to look at the engine, hear how she sounds.

Roman pulled his bee smoker out of the trunk, a bag of dry grass clippings to use in it, looked up at me and said, "But we beekeepers know that the most important part of a car is the trunk. You need a big trunk to haul around those deep honey-supers and all the supplies you need."

I nodded, smiled back. Roman had forgotten more about beekeeping than I knew, yet he treated me like an equal. It was "*we* beekeepers." Roman made me feel good. He not only showed me how to run the bees out of the top supers, he made me feel important. Roman knew how to handle people.

So it was natural later, when I went to see Roman in the nursing home, that we talked about bees. I would tell him about my hives, how they were doing, ask questions.

He sat there in his wheelchair, listened to my chatter, not responding, a vision of patience. In the several years that I visited Roman, he never said a word to me. If I went on too long, he would quietly close his eyes, signaling that I was rambling. So I would take the hint, slow down, come to silence. Sometimes I too closed my eyes, and we dreamed in silence.

Roman spent three years at Greencroft Nursing Home in Goshen, Indiana. He did not receive many visitors. Why? Some of us were busy. Some said they liked to remember Roman when he was active, strong, athletic. I guess they thought a silent Roman, a weak Roman, was not Roman.

How strange. In a wheelchair, silent, motionless, did he turn into someone else? Of course not. Roman in the nursing home was a person. He never became nameless protoplasm.

Sitting there, I wonder how much he heard. Perhaps far more than we realized. What happy memories were stirred by ones who came? And there were faithful friends. There were his children, grandchildren, brothers and sisters, and good wife Shirley. Did their visits lighten a long, long day?

Did a contact, the sight of someone he had not seen for ages, set his spirit free from the wheelchair? Perhaps his responses were inward, not outward. Hidden, not visible.

I remember Roman for his contribution to Goshen College. He gave thirty-seven years of his life to that institution, influenced thousands of students whose lives he touched as instructor, athletic director, coach. He was actively involved in church camping, gave hours to it at a time when church camps and camping were pretty worldly. Roman was a pioneer.

Roman was in Costa Rica, with his wife Shirley, when he had his second heart attack, just seven years after the first. There was bypass surgery in 1977, a large stroke a bit later. From that he largely recovered. Then a decline. Was it a series of small strokes, was it Alzheimer's disease, that sent Roman to the nursing home three years ago?

Regardless, every day he was there, he was someone, a real person. Lack of communication does not dehumanize. It does not make a person worthless, unsuitable to visit, inanimate. Sometimes, when I had only a few minutes but was in the area, I would enter his room, kneel beside his wheelchair, close my eyes, thank God for Roman. I touched God easier when I touched Roman. Roman helped to make the contact. Roman was a conductor.

I did not always leave Roman with joy, feeling good, pious, proud, happy with myself because I made the noble sacrifice. Once, on a bright sunshiny day, I took Roman outside. He seemed to resist me all the way, refusing to keep his feet up, often dragging one, impeding our wheelchair progress. It was discouraging.

Later we reentered the nursing home. I knelt beside the wheelchair. With a burst of strength, Roman reached out and pushed me away. I should have rejoiced at all the energy flowing through the synapses. I should have felt glad at his display of emotions, at the vigor of his reaction. Instead, my first thought was for myself, and I felt self-pity.

Visiting Roman was like visiting the psychiatrist. Sometimes you saw the selfishness that lies so shallow within, the pride so easily scratched. And you were shamed by the pity you felt for yourself. The Romans of the world have the right to have feelings, to experience love, anger, disappointment, grief, joy.

Roman was always a fighter, even in dying. When

another massive stroke struck in January, he did not surrender without a struggle. For a full ten days he fought the same good fight physically that he fought spiritually. Roman always maximized his Christianity, his spiritual race. He was no quitter on the basketball floor or on the hospital bed.

I am happy for the little time I spent with Roman. I wish it had been more. It was profitable time, prime time. Visiting Roman was visiting Jesus.

That is not a misprint. It is a clear application of Matthew 25 where Jesus speaks of those in prison, those hungry, thirsty, strangers, naked, sick. Jesus identified with the lonely, the needy, those in nursing homes. He said, "Inasmuch as ye have done it unto one of the least of these my brethren, ye have done it unto me" (Matt. 25:40, KJV)

So now you know of my own selfish reason for occasionally stopping at Room 84, Greencroft Nursing Home, Goshen, Indiana.

It gave me a chance to see Jesus.

VIII

A Partner Helps Smooth the Aging Wrinkles

Anna Mae and I married a bit late, both of us past the quarter-century mark. We married for better or for worse: I never had it better, she never had it worse. I am not just being humble. I thank God for a wife who has had the grace to love me, to stand by me, to gently guide as I tried to lead. She allowed me to write, extending her mothering to cover my lack of fathering.

When we married in 1947, a burgeoning world population was not an issue. So we had five children in ten years, without feeling sinful or embarrassed. They were good, tender-hearted, fun-loving, hard-working children, children who met God.

In marrying, parenting, and grandparenting, one experiences laughter and tears. Some of the laughter and tears are too personal to share. But Anna Mae and I will share a slice or two of our lives together. She winces at being mentioned in print. But it is impossible to be silent about one who has shared and endured what will have been, in 1997, a half century of life together.

As one ages, it's nice to have a partner walk with you into the ever-changing adventure which is the future. One cannot see around coming corners, but they become less fearsome if another holds your hand.

Marriage Enrichment
for Ancients

The programs were placed in our church mailboxes the Sunday before the seminar was scheduled. I quickly read the printed lines and scanned the seventy or so cubbyholes before me. Ah, here was one, there another. The programs, printed on brilliant red paper, were easily spotted. Most were in the boxes of young couples. A few middle-agers had them, but no true ancients like Anna Mae and myself.

I sighed in the church foyer. Was it a good idea to sign up? We like the leaders. That was a good reason. So we said yes. Was that the only reason? Probably not. Never having been to a marriage-enrichment affair, we felt some natural curiosity.

We were married almost forty years—and five children—ago. The nest was empty. Why rock the boat since the sailing had not been too bad? We would scarcely go another forty. If we did, I would be an even one hundred. Well, it might be a goal to shoot at. At one hundred I could get a birthday card from some U. S. president.

I think the idea started in our cluster. Our church

cluster was a small group, basically made up of people in their forties and fifties, and a few like us in our sixties or older. We knew one another well, were open, shared, spoke up, did things together. One couple had been to several marriage-enrichment meetings. They recommended it. They would go again. Could we make it a cluster activity? Three couples decided to try.

Attending such a marriage seminar opened one up to gossip. Were things that bad? Was it a last-ditch effort? Well, let others talk. We who attended such weekends were honest. It mattered not how good the marriage; it could always be improved. Some couples say they never quarrel. They insist their marriage has been one long, perfect honeymoon. They are either stretching the truth, are emotionless, or are out of step with reality.

There were four sessions scheduled for the weekend. We would learn how the other half lived. We would find out if we were the only odd couple on the block.

The sessions centered in the theme "Becoming One." The four subtitles were: "Why does it have to hurt so much?" "How we decide which one." "How can better communication help?" "One step at a time." It sounded like a lot of meat. It might contain a bit of gristle. But we went, attended all four sessions, and were the oldest couple there. The youngest pair was married less than a year. One divorcee attended.

I went planning to keep my mouth shut except for eating. I broke my vow the first session and was one of the more loquacious people attending. The leaders were talented but may have been surprised at seeing the likes of us present. They handled us with aplomb.

How did the marriage enrichment affect me, the old curmudgeon, male chauvinist par excellence, a member of the school that preceded the old school? Well, the best way to judge any husband is to ask his wife. But she refused to be interviewed. I will, therefore, speak for myself.

I found it a worthwhile investment of twenty dollars. It provided a bench mark, a spot against which to measure marriage progress. It offered a place to admit failures. It was a time to listen, to pray, and share with others.

There is usefulness in group therapy, and marriage enrichment can be that. To see another become vulnerable and survive gives one fresh courage. It is a step in one's spiritual journey.

There was a time set apart for spouses to talk. This is hard to do around one's busy home schedule, when husbands and wives pass like ships in the night. Anna Mae and I were doing this together. I was finding time for it, not begrudging the thirteen precious hours of time I surrendered. If I did it once, maybe I could do it again.

In others' comments, in fishbowl observations, in the telling of family stories, in recitation of the best of times, the worst of times, I saw myself. One did not say, "Ah, there but for the grace of God, go I." One said, "Ah, there because of my own lack of grace, go I." My faults were highlighted more than my perfections.

We were not at church. I did not approach the marriage-enrichment seminar as a religious service. But Anna Mae did. She saw it as church, a worship experience. So during the thirteen hours, she wore a prayer veiling.

Once in our denomination, it was the common practice for all the women in a church worship service to wear a simple, white, net-like head covering in accordance to Paul's instructions found in 1 Corinthians 11. At the time of our marriage enrichment, the practice was melting away like an ice cube on a hot stove.

Anna Mae took our involvement seriously, and it moved me. Her simple act humbled me, spoke to me. It reminded me of my weaknesses, her strengths, our togetherness, our equality in Christ Jesus, our mutual submission before him. There was a sweetness, a tenderness, an affirmation in the act that softened, enriched, challenged me.

After the closing communion service, I kissed my wife. It seemed fitting, proper, good.

So am I now perfect? Thirteen hours of marriage enrichment and I come out Mr. Marriage Dynamite? Do I now travel the matrimonial circuit, restoring foundering and splitting unions, the James Dobson of the Midwest?

Not quite. Not by a long shot. But I signed up with the same woman for another forty years. That should say something.

The Greyhound Escapade

On a life-crisis list, *separation* must surely rank high. I should know. During that summer, my wife and I separated. It was a friendly affair, no hard feelings. It was still traumatic, at least for me. After all, when you are married for three decades and counting, a separation does not fall into the same category as stopping the evening newspaper.

But we could not agree. Our youngest son, Tim, was to graduate from Western Washington University in June. He invited his parents to attend the exercises, promising to understand if we could not make it. I looked at my summer schedule, the distance to the Pacific Coast, our bank account, and the two tired four-cylinder cars in the garage. I suggested we sit this trip out.

But not Anna Mae. Would I care if she went by herself? Seeing her absent for no more than a week at most, I knew I could survive. And she deserved a week away from me. Okay. I visualized her flying the friendly skies with United.

Not so. A good steward of our money, a fine rider, capable of curling up on a dime and going to sleep, she would go by bus. I protested—too tiresome, too long. But I had preached pinching the pennies so frequently she was indoctrinated. She insisted on going by bus. Selah.

In planning to leave the driving to Greyhound, Anna Mae learned of the thirty-day pass. That turned out to be my nemesis. For $346.45, she purchased a book of tickets that could take her anyplace in the United States in thirty days. It cost little more than a round trip to her original destination in western Washington. That sold her. The plan began to germinate—a plan that would overwhelm me before it reached total fruition.

Anna Mae purchased her thirty-day pass a bit early, so she could use it to travel to Iowa for a funeral of an aunt. But that meant ten days between that trip and when our son graduated. Her commitment to good stewardship ran rampant. It created a fever. Would this not be a good time to visit her brother on Long Island? I ruminated. Then I shrugged, "Why not?" My assent was too easy. It encouraged her.

And when East, would it not be nice to also visit our second son near Washington, D. C.? I had visited him when east on business the summer before. So why should she not do it this summer? My shrug was weaker, but I answered, "It seems fair." Agreed.

Then like Abraham bargaining with God in Genesis 18, she said, "After Tim graduates, I could visit our friends near Sacramento, California."

Before I could react, she added triumphantly, "I

will already be West. The pass is good for thirty days, and the trip south will cost us nothing."

But what would it cost me in lonely hours isolated at County Road 13? She said nothing of that. I had no more energy left for shoulder shrugging. I simply said, "I guess it makes sense." What kind of a Pandora's box had been opened?

In a few days, she dropped another bomb. "Coming back from California, I could take the southern route east and visit Loren's folks [our daughter's in-laws] in Oklahoma."

I knew exactly how God felt when Abraham artfully persuaded him in Genesis 18:32 (NIV), "May the Lord not be angry, but let me speak just once more." I did not wait for her to hammer me with my own stewardship mallet. I did not wait for her to say without guile, "It will cost no more, and I should get full value out of the pass."

By reflex my head nodded, "Of course, visit Loren's folks." Through glazed eyes I saw the empty days stretching ahead, myself standing in line at McDonald's, Wendy's, and Arby's. I was trapped by my own philosophy: "Always try to get your money's worth."

So that summer, especially June, was an odd one. Anna Mae was home only sporadically during the thirty days. She would bob in to see that I still had clean shirts and underwear, that I was washing the dishes and sweeping the front room. After a quick inspection, she headed out to make another bus connection. I was beginning to shake my fist at every Greyhound bus I saw.

But the thirty days had to end eventually. From Oklahoma, Anna Mae called. If she went through Indianapolis, instead of Chicago, she could catch a bus to Marion and visit with our daughter there. She wanted to stay overnight, but the bus pass would have expired. Would I come to Marion and pick her up? By this time I was trained like Pavlov's dog. "Yes."

What did the summer teach me? Several things. My affinity for paper plates increased with geometric progression as time moved through June. When old, living by yourself can make you older. The house was so empty I began to carry on animated conversations with the dog. At night the bed was empty and wide. In the morning my coffee cup was dismally empty.

My male chauvinism suffered a sharp decline. Anna Mae managed transfers in Chicago and New York City with poise and assurance. In New York she moved from the large bus depot via taxi to Pennsylvania Railroad Station and located the proper Long Island train. She arrived safely at Hicksville, where her brother David Moyer lives. One missed bus would have let me express pity. I didn't get even that.

The chief thing I learned was that the one who said "Absence makes the heart grow fonder" was a knowledgeable person. I've also heard that immediately after my wife completed her summer itinerary, Greyhound raised the price of its thirty-day pass. To me that's understandable.

At Tender Age Zero

The walnut lies on my desk, the hull still around it. I picked it up one July 23. It fell from a young walnut tree at the edge of the valley below Plow Creek Farm near Tiskilwa, Illinois.

The day was hot and shining when I picked it up, an afterthought following the ceremony. Now the walnut is my prop, my reminder.

We had been there because of the telephone call that came the night before. "We wanted you to know, but we will certainly understand if you cannot come."

But we wanted to be there. So we canceled plans to go to a wedding and went to a funeral instead. Five hours of driving lay between us and them.

It was unusual, the whole experience. We had not known the dead. Just an hour before the service, we had our first view of him. Like a tiny doll, he lay in his burial crib. After only twenty-four weeks of growth, he had seen day and could not cope with the abrupt change from his mother's body. Soon after we saw him for the first and last time, the plain, unpainted, unvarnished box was sealed.

We stood with thirty or so other friends of the young couple. The pine coffin rested at the edge of the open grave, the rich chocolate earth piled beside it. I wept for the young parents. She sat on a bench beside the grave, still weak from the emergency cesarean.

I listened to the quiet words of the young man in charge of the service. I heard the songs and saw the joy leavening sadness in the faces around me. It is not that they do not care, it is just that they know so well that "if only for this life we have hope in Christ, we are to be pitied more than all men . . . in Christ all will be made alive" (1 Cor. 15:19, 22, NIV).

My mind fluttered from the service. Doug and Cindy had been married less than a year. They looked forward with such joy to the new life that stirred within. Then a week before July 23, while vacationing on the East Coast, totally unexpected difficulties arose. Far from home, they made a hurried thirty-mile ride at night to the hospital. Their baby boy struggled for an hour but could not live.

I came back to the quiet Illinois valley. Cindy was singing a song she had written.

JONATHAN
Little son, many nights I'd rock you gently,
     Feel you moving deep within my being.
Precious child, gift of heaven, we received so much from you,
     Never thought your life would be so brief.

Torn from my heart,
Torn from our loving arms.

Jonathan, you are with the one who caused us all to be,
  He now holds you in eternal arms.
Precious son, gift of heaven, miracle that we beheld,
  We return you to his loving care.

  Child of our love,
  Child of our Father.

In our hearts we carry you, little one we'll see no more.
  Till the day we all are whole again.
Angel child, bridge to heaven, sign of life's fragility,
  Now we rest you in God's merciful care.

  Child of our love,
  Child of our Father.

Jonathan, a gift of heaven, miracle that we beheld
  We now rest you in God's merciful care.

There were other testimonies. Twice the child's father spoke, with confidence, courage, and acceptance. Then the wee coffin was gently lowered into the warm earth. Doug, the father, held a shovel of earth to Cindy beside him. She lifted a tiny handful of soil from the metal and threw it on the coffin.

Other hands took the shovels. I noted two men talking quietly together, looking at me. They approached me, holding out a shovel, an invitation without spoken word. I took the shovel and thrust it deeply into the earth. I could scarcely see. One shovelful was all I could manage.

Today the walnut tree stands close to Jonathan Noah and keeps its silent vigil, shading, protecting, sheltering, watching. We thank God for what he does to us who sorrow and come to him for healing.

Yes, the experience was simple, yet rich. It was the burial of our first grandson, Jonathan Noah Baker.

Weekend Rendezvous

I gently replaced the phone on the hook. It was a call out of the past, forty years in the past. It transported me back to when I was a college student. Was it that long since we had seen each other?

The caller had learned I was coming East for a weekend and wanted to renew acquaintanceship. Could we get together? On the spur of the moment, I had agreed.

I was thoughtful, a bit excited, more than a bit. The heart pounded, the blood ran faster. Married nearly forty years. Now this telephone call that reawakened the past. I remembered everything about that relationship. It was premarriage, five children ago, but still vivid.

The weeks snailed past me. The anticipated weekend finally came.

Friday night I flew East. Embers long covered were glowing.

Saturday I was at the church where I was to hold a Sunday school seminar. My telephone caller would pick me up there. We would be together for part of the weekend, overnight arrangements already verified. Would we recognize one another? I thought so. How could we forget? Would the past be recalled, old memories revived?

I was in the church basement setting up the room for the first meeting, when I heard the voice outside the door. I recognized it, kept my head down, almost frightened that the moment was here.

I looked up. Wonderful. Unchanged after all these years.

*   *   *

The above material was contained on a handout sheet I passed out during a writers' conference. It was part of my input. I asked those attending to suggest how the short article might end. It was a Christian writers' group, so they wanted it to end correctly. They treated it seriously, for I had told them it was the truth, not fiction.

And it was. The call actually came to me, I went East, met the caller, we were together for part of the weekend. I did leave out one thing, though. The caller was Earl Schmidt, a college roommate of mine at Goshen College during the year 1939-1940.

Thus the workshop group did not know that my caller was male. They were unaware that he simply wanted me to visit their home in Biglerville, Pennsylvania over the weekend and meet his wife and children.

My writer friends, as you would expect, thought the caller was an old girlfriend. They worried about me. They were disappointed in the way I handled things. They wanted to extricate me from the possible affair. I did not ask how many saw the caller as a female. But I am certain the majority did. Why?

I had given them no untruths; I had but set the stage. Their imagination completed the drama. Their minds spelled it out thus because that is the type of world in which we live. It is a world of unfaithfulness, of married people having affairs, of divorces, of premarital sex, of moral looseness.

What has all of this to do with us, the readers of this page? Many of us are married. A number of us are mature and have more of life behind us than before us. We are conservative in morals, I trust, taking Paul's advice to overseers as suitable for ourselves. In 1 Timothy 3:2, we see that such are to be "above reproach, the husband of but one wife, temperate, self-controlled." I presume a woman is likewise to be the wife of but one husband. Selah.

I realize there are certain ages, like the forties, when people see life escaping them and marital infidelities become more prevalent. But there is scarcely any age that is exempt from the possibility.

One might look at some of us pre-Depression ancients, never confused with Hollywood models, and wonder if concern is necessary.

I know of too many real-life illustrations, Christian and otherwise, to eliminate any of us. It is a world in which affairs are common, ministers fail, sexual freedom is promulgated. Such a world could use the following:

(1) Be happy, even proud, if your monogamous rec-

ord is intact. Married four-plus decades, there is no blemish on my fidelity record. I'm glad.

(2) Realize not everyone is doing it. The devil sells us a bill of goods and says they are. They aren't.

(3) Fight divorce with love, honesty, and faithfulness. I say this kindly, recognizing that many of my divorced friends fought it, preferring a happy marriage.

(4) Be a warm-fuzzy thrower. Toss frequent fuzzies to your spouse—he or she must be doing some things right.

(5) Read and reread the Bible. Its teachings and standards are clear. Know them, follow them. Review your marriage vows periodically. Recreate the joy with which they were made. Keep them.

IX

Heavenly Retirement

We are great at discussing the weather, politics, religion, athletics, cars, television programs, and other controversial subjects. We don't talk so freely about death, which is a rather sure thing—you can argue about going, but you go. My parents prepared for my birth. But they pretty much left it up to me to prepare for my death.

Cases of people escaping death are somewhat limited. Enoch was a man who walked with God and "God took him away" (Gen. 5:24). Elijah left in somewhat more spectacular fashion. A fiery, chariot-style limousine whisked him directly through the pearly gates, bypassing both coroner and funeral home attendants (2 Kings 2:11). Dying appears fairly normal for the rest of us.

I hope, having read thus far, you have concluded I belong to that odd breed of religious cats known as "born-again Christians." Right on! Rebirth is solid preparation for dying—but is dwarfed by God's plans for our future living (John 14:1-4).

Death is mysterious. So, if we are honest, there is trembling mixed with our curiosity. I think Jesus will still every tremble. Meanwhile, it would be stupid not to prepare for the inevitable.

Honest Fear, Quiet Assurance

"Bob Baker, I believe you are afraid of growing old."

Moses Slabaugh so tagged me back in the 1970s, when I was in my fifties. I was a guest in his home for a few days. He was an interim pastor in Illinois, and I was at his church as a weekend speaker. The man pulls no punches. Those who know Moses can hear him say the words. He is not a man to hide his analysis under a bushel of tact. He speaks bluntly, tartly, meaningfully, with keen insight.

I am not sure what prompted his diagnosis. I do recall somewhat my defense and still feel much the same. I do not fear old age. I do fear the decreasing lack of earthly time available to me. My wife, the best analyst a husband has at his disposal, shakes her head. She despairs as she watches my frantic efforts to meet work quotas in a daily rat race that the rats seem to be winning. She has learned to stop and smell the roses I am so desperately planting.

Do I have a legitimate fear of growing old? At age sixty, I first checked out my life expectancy.

Back then they suggested I should not count on much more than sixteen additional years. So it looked like the old hulk might make it to age seventy-six.

I checked again when I was sixty-nine, just to see if things might have improved. Good thing I did! *The Statistical Abstract of the United States* (109th edition, 1989) raised the possibility of my stringing it out until I was eighty, depending on such variables as sex, state, race.

I was thankful for commutation of my death sentence to the year 2,000. I think I'll look up life expectancy more frequently since the odds seem to get better when you do. I presume, however, there is a limit to everything, including years of life remaining.

Into that ever-narrowing, fast-decreasing slot of time, I must work in a number of items. These range all the way from painting the front room to writing the great American novel. New items and establishing new priorities for old ones have me treadmilling at times just to stay even.

So I wonder, "Will I make it?" When the death summons comes, will the angel find me working on a manuscript as a plane takes me to a Sunday school workshop, my briefcase crammed with books and pamphlets that must be read, a paint color chart in my coat pocket?

"Moses Slabaugh, for that reason I do fear growing old. Is that wrong? Worse yet, is it sin?"

There are other reasons I fear advancing age. At the end of old age is death, the River Styx to be crossed, no round trip tickets. Death is a nonrepeatable event, with no trial runs. I'm a little fuzzy on what the experience is like.

The unknown is feared by many. True, the Bible gives us a preview of heaven, but it's still quite a jump from here to there. Death has few rational takers, people crowding to get to the head of the line. Like Hezekiah, another fifteen years doesn't look bad to me.

Some of us may also fear the loss of physical prowess. We must switch from push lawn mowers to riding ones. We must allow the younger ones to do the spring cleaning at church. We must reduce the size of the garden. The joy of working, of sex, of being independent are good. So we legitimately fear hitting the physical skids of the sixties, seventies, and beyond. We're afraid we will slide into a convalescent home, become a burden.

There's another caution light that begins to flash with increasing tempo as the years roll around. As we review our personal lives, relive the manuscripts we have written, we see the smudged pages. We see words crossed out, uneven margins, editorial comments written by God in red, calling attention to errors, both minor and gross.

Our debts appear to exceed our assets. Our chance to balance the budget seems less likely. We need a few more centuries of time. Even then, I see St. Peter scanning mine, saying slowly, "Well, you made it, but barely. Please step through the side door when nobody is looking."

But I need not only fear. I can do something about my fear.

First, I need to be careful that my dread of unfinished projects is not born of egotism, of a desire to get into the new volume of *The Mennonite Encyclopedia.* The great American novel can be finished in heaven, if it even needs to be written.

Certainly the unknown is fearful. But I like the word *awe* a bit better than *fear.* Let me see the unknown from that perspective, taking the stance of the explorer. In each of us still lies that boyish, girlish dream to see, to find, to discover, to experience new worlds.

So let me move from earth to heaven with awe accompanying me. Death is simply the vehicle. The Christ to whom I cling in life will not desert me when the shadows are longer, the valley deeper, the river wider.

I can scarcely take enough vitamin E to escape declining physical strength. And it may be a causeless worry, a senseless fear. God may say, "That's all, Bob," through a sudden coronary or with a massive trailer truck gaining the right of way over my small Honda.

One fear I can dispose of. It's the fear of not balancing the budget, of having the "bad works" column outweigh the "good works" column. Or, put another way, "Have I earned sufficient brownie points?"

The devil loves to make me feel guilty, sucker me into questioning, but God has loving answers of grace in the Bible. Among them, I cherish Paul's advice to the church at Ephesus: "And God raised us up with Christ. . . . For it is by grace you have been saved, through faith . . . it is the gift of God—not by works, so that no one can boast" (Eph. 2:6-8, NIV).

These are gentle, comforting words for one who is task oriented. According to James, works and faith are both important, but faith effectively continues long after our works have faded into obscurity. Isaiah 64:6 labels my "good works" as "filthy rags." It reads the same in both the King James and New International versions. Wow! What a wonderful, deserved put-down on any résumé of accomplishments I file for heavenly consideration.

Nevertheless, from here until God closes the books and says, "Come," I want always to work as hard as I can and continue to praise him. I want to grow older gracefully, humbly, with full assurance, not with dragging feet, wringing hands, wailing voice.

Moses Slabaugh, I trust I have spoken to your observation and qualified my "fear" of growing old.

Common Sense Preparations

On that day forty years ago, only the screen door stood between the two salesmen and myself. I feared that even this thin, sievelike barrier would soon be removed. The two of them, ganging up on me, were selling cemetery lots, my name having been given them by a fellow teacher. Their arguments were firm, persuasive, psychologically intended to beat me down. I stood there helpless. I wanted to say "No," to be rid of them. But I didn't.

Then my wife came to the door to see what was keeping me from other duties. Quickly she gathered data, sizing up what was taking place on both sides of the screen door. She surmised my weak position and said quickly, decisively. "We are not in the market at present for cemetery lots. We can't afford to live, let alone die."

In a moment, the surprised and taken-aback salesmen folded up their brochures, and I was free. My wife provided the galloping cavalry that arrived in the nick of time.

We were still in our twenties, and her statement of financial precariousness was quite correct. The children came quickly, and the teaching profession at that time paid meagerly. We were struggling.

Now we are in our seventies. Although dying is certainly not my first area of choice for advanced planning, it is time we ascertain that certain groundwork (no pun intended) has been laid. What preparations have we made for changing our status from present to absent?

Obviously, to me, at the top of the list is a spiritual decision. Long ago, both Anna Mae and I as preteenagers signed on the dotted line. The contract is still in effect. We made certain commitments to follow Jesus. It was the best preparation for dying we could have made; it is our spiritual insurance policy.

I take a great deal of pleasure in reading Jesus' own words in John 14:2-3 (NIV): "In my Father's house are many rooms. . . . I am going there to prepare a place for you. . . . I will come back and take you to be with me." It beats my teacher-retirement plan, Social Security, and the IRA we started forty years too late.

But, of course, not everyone leaves at the same time, and those staying prefer not to start tidying things up from scratch. So we have initiated a few other preparations but still have several items to clear up, time permitting. Writing this section is a gentle reminder of what's yet hanging fire.

We finally made a will. It was something we had put off far too long. I called a former student of mine, now a practicing attorney, and set up an appointment. In his air-conditioned office, on a hot

July day, we got the job done.

I like to read the will. I smile over the legal language. But I save my biggest smile for the last page. There the witnesses testify "that the Testator was of sound mind." It was nice of them to capitalize me, the Testator, and to judge me sane.

The pitch made by the cemetery salesmen for our plot of ground has still not been finalized. We do have an acre of ground where we live, but I presume the neighbors would object if we settled down and were planted back by the tree house. So we are looking elsewhere.

For some twenty years I have been mowing a little half-acre-or-less, country cemetery that our family rescued from the wilderness. It contains the graves of my great-grandparents, and my great-great-grandparents on my mother's side. So it's family. The last burial there was in the 1930s, but there is still space.

A preliminary inquiry to the gentleman who holds the plot records was favorable. His ancestors are buried there, too, and he appreciates my lawn work. He thinks things can be worked out, but I would like to get it down on paper. Who knows— for my faithful mowing I may get a bargain price!

"Funeral services are incomplete at this time" is the statement appearing in some obituary accounts in the local paper. So it is with Anna Mae and me. We need to do more planning for actual services. Basically, we want things kept simple. A bronze casket will not be necessary, and, for myself, I prefer the old blue suit with the slash pockets.

At the time I don't suppose anyone will ask me, but, personally, I vote now for a simple church service. For the singing, I prefer "Lift Your Glad Voices" to "Come, Ye Disconsolate." A short, snappy, stimulating sermon will suffice. Minimum flowers.

Well, as you can see, I've made a little progress since first approached by the grave sellers.

O, yes, one final thing. Please don't talk about my "interment" (burial in the ground). It sounds too much like "internment" (confining prisoners). To me, death is really freedom, not imprisonment.